The Dramatic Unity
of *Huckleberry Finn*

George C. Carrington, Jr.

The Dramatic Unity
of *Huckleberry Finn*

Ohio State University Press : Columbus

Library of Congress Cataloging in Publication Data

Carrington, George C
    The dramatic unity of "Huckleberry Finn"

    Includes bibliographical references and index.
        1. Clemens, Samuel Langhorne, 1835–1910. The adventures of Huckleberry Finn.
I. Title.
PS1305.C3   813'.4   76-939
ISBN 0-8142-0238-1

Contents

Introduction

The hundreds of books and articles on *Huckleberry Finn* have failed to answer a basic question about the novel: Does the ending belong to the book? Answering "No" as many critics of the book have done puts students of American literature in an embarrassing position. Almost all such critics consider *Huckleberry Finn* not just an interesting novel, but a very great novel, one of the supreme American works of art. *PMLA*, the official publication of university English studies, has declared it a national treasure.[1] But many able critics have agreed that the ending of the "great American novel"[2] seriously violates its unity. (One critic would omit the beginning, too.)[3] The ending of *Huckleberry Finn* being a quarter of the novel, we are left with a radically flawed treasure, as if *Hamlet* had a bungled fifth act. This situation does not seem to bother many critics, but I think it should. Works of the first order should stand up to the most searching examination. Either we should establish that *Huckleberry Finn* is unified, even if we dislike its mode of unity, or we should let the present towering reputation of the novel lapse, and call it a partial failure like *Pierre*—a significant partial failure, and a

greater achievement than the successes of many minor
artists, but a partial failure just the same. And no matter
how one defines "partial," a partial failure is not a success.

Rather than drive the question into a Thoreauvian
corner, it is pleasant to let the matter rest. American
literature has so few indisputable masterpieces (as
admirers of English literature rather enjoy pointing out)
that upholders of our literature are tempted to inflate the
virtues and play down the faults of our candidates. But,
seizing the nettle, I have looked in *Huckleberry Finn*
for what Twain himself, in a letter to Howells, called
"the nameless something . . . the subtle something"[4]
that accounts, he thought, for the nature and the life of a
true work of literary art. I have reached conclusions that
may help readers in the eternal dialectic that is the critical
life of a major work of art.

Before I outline my argument I should deal with some
of my assumptions, some possible objections to them, and
some critical approaches that I think get in a way of a
full understanding of *Huckleberry Finn* and its ending,
whether that full understanding involves my conclusions
or not. First, I assume that every word of the novel can be
taken seriously and that Twain (as he suggests in his
prefatory notes) knew what he was doing. As David Lodge
has said, "Apart from the possibility of textual corruption
having occurred in the process of printing (where the
critic must rely upon the assistance of textual scholarship),
we may, in citing a reliable text and sticking to it, be
confident that we are dealing with an artistic whole."[5]
I use the Houghton Mifflin paperback text of *Huckleberry
Finn*, which follows Twain's carefully prepared first
edition, and in which the major corruptions (the chapter
titles and the word *The* in the title) have been eliminated.

An argument based on piety toward the author's text must face the *ad hominem* counterattack, which places Twain in the class of Wolfe and Kerouac, Dionysian writers who knew less about their works than critics know. Bernard De Voto, who crushed Wolfe with the comment "Genius is not enough," tried to crush the ending of *Huckleberry Finn* by calling it "extemporized burlesque."[6] Wolfe's surly reactions to De Voto's attack suggest that the critic was right in that case; but Twain was not present to defend his own novel, and the idea that the ending of *Huckleberry Finn* is careless improvising or extemporizing has gained wide acceptance. De Voto's attack begs the question when he talks about improvising, but he is on more acceptable ground when he criticizes the ending for being irrelevant. Perhaps De Voto took surface effect for totality of meaning and failed to dig for that "nameless something." "To string incongruities and absurdities together in a wandering and sometimes purposeless way" was to Twain the way to form "the American art," the humorous story; "to . . . seem innocently unaware that they are absurdities" was the stance to be taken by the artist.[7] There may be a moral lurking here for the student of Twain's fiction. "You were all there for him, but he was not all there for you," said Howells, who for many years knew Twain as well as any man ever did, that is, not very well.[8]

Twain was fully capable of shrewd professional self-criticism. His comments on the rewriting of *Those Extraordinary Twins* suggest that he was aware of structural problems of the sort that bother critics of *Huckleberry Finn*. When he wanted to, Twain could turn out well-made novels—*The Prince and the Pauper* and *Joan of Arc*, for example. "How to Tell a Story" and the essays on Cooper show that Twain had decided opinions on technique and craftsmanship; we may disagree with those opinions, but not with the fact that he had them and was proud of them. He was capable of hopelessly bad judgments of his own manuscripts, like the burlesque *Hamlet* that he wrote in the summer of 1881.[9] But just as Clemens distinguished sharply between his public (including semiprivate) and his really private behavior, between reading Browning with the ladies in the parlor and reading *1601* with his cronies in the billiard room, so Mark Twain, his literary persona, distinguished between his improvisations and his real work. What is important about the burlesque *Hamlet* is not Twain's passing enthusiasm for it but his later and permanent rejection of it. De Voto is right in saying that Twain *wrote* "improvisations," unplanned verbal doodlings, but wrong in saying that Twain *published* them. In judging *Huckleberry Finn* we must concentrate on the relevant fact, the published novel.

There is no use speculating on the novel as it could have been written or as we think it should have been written. Henry James put the critic's obligation very well: "We don't know what people might give us that they don't—the only thing is to take them on what they do and to allow them absolutely and utterly their conditions." It is all too easy, as the history of Twain criticism shows, not to allow him his "conditions"—beginning with his own respect for the published work—and not to concentrate on what he "does" under those conditions.

Any character we draw for Twain, from white Uncle Remus to dirty old man, can be supported from his works and behavior. He had passionate opinions on many sides of everything and gave them forth lavishly. It is

dangerously easy to see this writer of many ideas as a
worker with ideas, a controlled and self-critical
verbalizer in the modern tradition of Joyce, a builder
of logical systems—or, not finding such systems, to assume
that Twain was trying to create them and failing. Thus
many readings of *Huckleberry Finn*, especially those of
the 1950s and 1960s, torture the novel on the Procrustean
beds of modern criticism and modern intellectual
life. We apply our own terms to the novel, and if they
fail, we blame Twain. Much of the trouble in examining
Huckleberry Finn comes from demanding rigid consistency.
Some readers apply the formalist or "new critical"
concept of the work of art as a thing that radiates meaning
but is nevertheless basically a thing, composed of parts
whose harmony is brought into the work from fixed genres
or modes. Henry Nash Smith, author of the most
respected book on Twain's fiction, is upset because
"what had begun as a comic story developed incipiently
tragic implications contradicting the premises of comedy."[10]
A novel, that is, has no business breaking the rules of
generic consistency. Professor Smith analyzes this
situation generically, in terms of the effects of Twain's
triumph with Huck's point of view and with the
"vernacular" style of the novel. To Professor Smith
these triumphs posed "a new technical problem to which
there was no solution."[11] Rather than consider the
matter a violation, it might be better to see it as a
characteristic. The same critic complains that Tom
Sawyer, at the end of *Huckleberry Finn*, "has no tragic
dimension whatever,"[12] so that Twain violates the tragic
mood that was itself a violation of the original comic
mood of the novel. We can see here the limits of genre

criticism, which introduces unconsciously the idea of decorum and ignores the possibility of functional relationships that may incidentally be violations of decorum. "Pastoral" is another genre term the use of which results in a demand for rigidity. Once Huck gets onto Jackson's Island or out in midstream on the raft, he should stay there, it seems. (But perhaps Huck has reasons for moving, and Twain has reasons for moving him.) Genre operates negatively, too. The ending of the novel is often seen as "farce," which is taken as inferior to both "tragedy" and "comedy." No matter what he does, Twain is doubly damned. If shifting from comedy to tragedy is wrong, then shifting from comedy or tragedy to farce, the lowest of the low, is disgraceful. One critic attacks a reading of the ending as farce by saying, "Such a reading deprives *Huckleberry Finn* of any serious meaning."[13] In such a view farce is "low," not "serious"; it cannot tell us anything important about the human condition. But perhaps it can, and I will try to show that the farce in the ending of *Huckleberry Finn* does tell us something of great importance that should upset us.

American literature and American studies have in part tried to justify their existence as undergraduate academic fields with the claim that study of the materials of their fields makes the student a better person. The ending of *Huckleberry Finn* is a bother to supporters of this view. Huck seems to develop morally until in chapter 31 he becomes a truly noble figure, but within a few pages he has relapsed into clownishness, and the last chapter finds him about where he was at the beginning. To a moralistic critic, who wants Huck to help us stand

at moral attention forever, the ending is unendurable.
In a powerfully argued and widely influential essay
Professor Leo Marx maintains that the novel is a quest,
Huck is "the redemptive possibility of the human race,"
and the ending, violating both quest and possibility, is
outrageous. Professor Marx is so upset by this betrayal, as
he sees it, that he polarizes the ending in relation to
the body of the novel, and shows Huck changing from
a saint to a worm, who makes an "awestruck submission"
to Tom Sawyer.[14] Better than weakness and clowning
would be total failure, so we now have Professor John
Seelye's rewritten version of *Huckleberry Finn* in which
Jim dies and Huck is left in solitary despair.[15] Seelye's
Huck retains, throughout, that splendid "commitment to
freedom and spontaneity" that Henry Nash Smith finds
early in the novel in Twain's Huck.[16] Despite its
surface coarseness the Seelye version suggests the
neoclassic dictum that if a book is not "correct," it should
be rewritten.

But we must not reduce *Huckleberry Finn* to a tract,
unless it is clear that Twain wanted readers to see it as a
tract, and there is no strong evidence for that. Readers
of this novel have too often been "bettors" rather than
"spectators," to use W. B. Gallie's terms. The bettor,
being interested in one outcome only, has lost the
spectator's pure interest in the game itself, and, if it goes
against him, either turns away in disgust, or tries to
tamper with the game.[17] Or, to use a more literary image,
this approach to *Huckleberry Finn*, this using it rather
than studying it, is still linked to what Frank Kermode
calls the first two stages of man's use of the past, the
stages of ritual and pattern-finding, rather than the third

contemporary stage, in which we see that pattern-finding
is anthropocentric. "We are still not quite easy with
the third stage," says Kermode, providing a polite epitaph
for critics' distress about *Huckleberry Finn* and the
difficulties of its ending.[18]

To be "easy" with *Huckleberry Finn*, one must be like an
anthropologist entering a strange village in a strange
culture. The critic must force himself to let the novel
present itself, to let incidents and their effects cluster
into patterns that eventually form their own kind of whole,
with their own kind of effect. Speaking after the fact,
after letting the novel present itself, I find that I have a
structuralist study, that is, one that finds not just order
but order-making under an apparent disorder or
discontinuity. Structuralism as an intellectual movement
defies and indeed dislikes clear, rigid definition; it
prefers to see itself as an activity. Roland Barthes says
that "the goal of all structuralist activity, whether reflexive
[e.g., critical] or poetic, is to reconstruct an 'object' in
such a way as to manifest thereby the rules of functioning
(the 'functions') of the object. . . . The imitated object
makes something appear which remained invisible, or
if one prefers unintelligible in the natural object."[19]
That "something" (which recalls Twain's "nameless
something") may be called the "deep structure" of the
work. This "something" is "intellect added to object"; it
is what creating man adds when he fabricates "a world
which resembles the first [real] one, not in order to
copy it but to render it intelligible." What defines an art
or a work of art is "not the nature of the copied object
. . . (though this is a tenacious prejudice in all realism),
it is the fact that man adds to it in reconstructing it:
technique is the very being of all creation." The

structuralist activity is concerned with relations, with
the way in which the elements of the work function;
it is not concerned with the real or the rational (so that,
for example, it matters not if the structure be a nonobjective
work of art or a nonutilitarian human activity). Cultural
and artistic elements, "whatever their inner structure
and their extent, . . . have no significant existence
except by their frontiers," which define their relations.
From these basic elements and from classes of elements
the work, like a language, is generated by means of
repetition of the elements, or members of the same
class of elements, and their relationships—"stability" and
"regularity of assemblages," as Barthes puts it. The
inhabitant of a culture or the maker of a work of art
need have no idea that he is *homo significans*, a maker of
meaningful structures; in fact, the culture and the work of
art do better if the structural activity is unconscious.
Art in this sense is a "mantic activity," which "speaks"
meaning but does not name it. What it speaks is what
Barthes strikingly calls a *shudder*. The ancient,

> amazed by the *natural* in nature, . . . perceived in the vege-
> tal or cosmic order a tremendous *shudder* of meaning, to which
> he gave the name of a god: Pan. Subsequently, nature has
> changed, has become social. . . . But confronted with this
> social nature, which is quite simply culture, structural man is
> no different from the ancient Greek: he too listens for the
> natural in culture, and constantly perceives in it not so much
> stable, finite, "true" meanings as the shudder of an enormous
> machine which is humanity tirelessly undertaking to create
> meaning, without which it would no longer be human.

This presentation of the structuralist approach defines
the approach to *Huckleberry Finn* that I took intuitively
because no other approach was adequate. When I took

the materials of *Huckleberry Finn* in a literal or rational way,
then the book was confused and confusing, as most
critics have found it to be; but when I considered the
materials in terms of their relations, then I found patterns,
repetitions—Barthes's "stability" and "regularity of
assemblages." I found a book that speaks a meaning,
that presents "humanity tirelessly undertaking to create
meaning, without which it would no longer be human." I
did not find the book naming that meaning. I doubt
that Twain realized that his meaning was man's effort
to create meaning, or could have faced or named that point
when he wrote *Huckleberry Finn*, although he began to
fumble toward it in his old age, in works like *What
Is Man?*.

In the following pages I will try to speak in the language
of criticism what *Huckleberry Finn* "speaks" in the
language of fiction. First I will try to define what kind
of world Twainian man finds himself in and how he
reacts to his sense of that world. Then I will define the
mechanism, which I call "drama," by which man tries
to give his world stability and patterns, that is, to structure
it, to give it meaning, without which, as Barthes says and
Twain shows, man is "no longer human." Then I will
try to show that the whole novel, including the ending,
"speaks" that method, and is a structure of episodes
that lack surface connections but are intimately connected
on the level of deep structure—that is, are similar in
basic elements and are generated one from another by
consistent rules. Thus I will hope to prove that given
the world of this novel, Twainian man in it, and man's
structure-making efforts, the qualities of *Huckleberry
Finn* are inevitable, and the ending is necessary and right.

I assume that the reader of such a monograph as this has a sound knowledge of *Adventures of Huckleberry Finn*, a working knowledge of the Twain canon, and a copy of one of the many adequate editions of *Huckleberry Finn* available now. With such a reader in mind, I refer to the novel by chapter rather than by page. My quotations from the novel are from the edition of Henry Nash Smith (Boston: Houghton Mifflin, 1958).

1. "For Members Only," *PMLA* 72 (March 1967): A-4.

2. William Lyon Phelps applied this term to *Huckleberry Finn* in *Howells, James, Bryant, and Other Essays* (New York: Macmillan, 1924), p. 160.

3. Philip Young would omit the beginning too. See *Ernest Hemingway* (New York: Rinehart and Co., 1952), p. 196.

4. 16 January 1904, in Henry Nash Smith and William M. Gibson, eds., *Mark Twain-Howells Letters* (Cambridge, Mass.: Harvard University Press, 1960), 2:778.

5. *Language of Fiction: Essays in Criticism and Verbal Analysis of the English Novel* (London and New York: Columbia University Press, 1966), p. 38.

6. *Mark Twain's America* (1932; rpt. Boston: Houghton Mifflin, 1967), p. 312.

7. "How to Tell a Story," *The Writings of Mark Twain*, Stormfield Edition (New York and London: Harper, 1929), 24:267 (hereafter cited as Stormfield Ed.).

8. *My Mark Twain* (New York: Harper, 1910), p. 29.

9. Franklin R. Rogers, ed., *Mark Twain's Satires and Burlesques* (Berkeley and Los Angeles: University of California Press, 1967), pp. 8-9, 49-86.

10. *Mark Twain: The Development of a Writer* (Cambridge, Mass.: Harvard University Press, 1962), p. 114.

11. Ibid., pp. 113-14.

12. Ibid., p. 134.

13. Claude M. Simpson, *Twentieth Century Interpretations of "The Adventures of Huckleberry Finn"* (New York: Prentice-Hall, 1968), p. 3.

14. "Mr. Eliot, Mr. Trilling, and *Huckleberry Finn*," *American Scholar* 22 (Autumn 1953): 423-40.

15. *The True Adventures of Huckleberry Finn* (Evanston, Ill.: Northwestern University Press, 1969).

16. *Mark Twain: The Development of a Writer*, p. 122.

17. *Philosophy and the Historical Understanding*, 2d ed. (New York: Schocken Books, 1968), p. 56.

18. *The Sense of an Ending: Studies in the Theory of Fiction* (New York: Oxford University Press, 1967), p. 56.

19. All quotations from Barthes are from "The Structuralist Activity," trans. Richard Howard, in Richard and Fernand De George, eds., *The Structuralists from Marx to Levi-Strauss* (Garden City, N.Y.: Doubleday, 1972), pp. 149–54.

The Dramatic Unity
of *Huckleberry Finn*

The World of *Huckleberry Finn* and Man in It

I

The world that Mark Twain has imagined as the non-human basis of *Huckleberry Finn* is a world of disorder and chaos, but, being an imagined world, it is a structure of disorder and therefore orderly. To use Kenneth Burke's trick with italics, we have a model of *disorder* that is at the same time a *model* of disorder. The disorder is presented through a narrator who is incapable of perceiving order under the surface of the things and events he reports, as we see in the Grangerford episode, when order is thrust under his nose: "There was some books. . . . One was 'Pilgrim's Progress,' about a man that left his family it didn't say why. I read considerable in it now and then. The statements was interesting but tough" (chap. 17). Huck encounters the greatest Puritan literary embodiment of the Christian apocalyptic tradition, the central form-creating tradition of his culture, and he is baffled. He cannot even grasp the fact that *Pilgrim's Progress is* an organization, a fictional action. He perceives a beginning, a man leaving his family, without realizing what that means in itself or in relation to the rest of the book. He is not aware that he ought to know the meaning of the beginning without being told, or that, if he does not know it, he ought to try to figure it out. He does not look outward from the book to the world around him; certainly he sees no parallel between his own leaving of Pap and Mr. Christian's leaving of his family, no contrast between the Grangerfords' savage behavior and their ostentatious display of this book. *Pilgrim's Progress* is "interesting, but tough"—something is there, perhaps, and Huck is stimulated to dip into the book, but he is incompetent to find the meaning. In his narration, written a month or two later, he shows no curiosity about his failure. He drops the matter and goes on to finish his description of the Grangerford parlor.

Twain reinforces the point of this isolated but significant instance with the repeated ironical references to the snakeskin. As those references show, Huck and Jim think that they are pursuing some fate down the river. By handling that snakeskin, Huck violated, he believes, some mysterious law of nature and doomed Jim and himself to —what? We never find out. Huck does not tell us; he does not know, and cannot know, because there never was any such law of nature—there was only Huck's belief that there was. At the end Jim is freed and officially becomes a human being; Huck plans to go on being himself; and Tom Sawyer, Huck implies, is going to do the same. So perhaps one's fate is to exist and, as one who is being and not becoming, to imitate the "fate" of a John Marcher and have no fate. Santayana said that men like Twain could point to the flaws in the genteel tradition but could not abandon it because "they have nothing solid to put in its place."[1] "Nothing solid" and "no fate" are indeed what *Huckleberry Finn* offers us, without Huck's knowledge. Conventional causation ("fate") is replaced by random change; solidity is replaced by the mutability expressed in an image Huck uses twice—the constant "squshing" of a river bank undercut by the gnawing of the river (chaps. 21, 29).

The destruction of solidity, the creation of "squshiness," that is, the celebration of random activity and the denial of stasis and finality—these are at the heart of the world of *Huckleberry Finn* as it presents itself to the characters and to the reader. In postulating the universality of activity, often frenetic or destructive, Twain foreshadows the nightmare ending of *A Connecticut Yankee*, and in a later era the inexhaustible pointless creativity of the Satan-figures in the *Mysterious Stranger* manuscripts and the energy of argument in *What Is Man?* And in writing *Huckleberry Finn* itself, Twain demonstrated his principle of activity: he pigeonholed the manuscript more than once, and returned to it more than once before finally finishing it, thus maximizing the possible fuss.

This ever-active disorder I call "turbulence," a useful contemporary scientific term for the basic form of ordered disorder or orderly disorder in the universe. "Every system of 'statistical order,' if viewed in sufficiently broad perspective, will be found to be part (fluctuating and temporary though it may be) of a larger, more inclusive system of turbulence." The "systems of 'statistical order' " that constitute the scientist's reality tend to "interpenetrate" each other, thus putting stress on each other and causing

a breakdown into "turbulence."[2] In order to describe
natural turbulence, the scientist must analyze in terms of
process, and the critic in his efforts to understand *Huckleberry Finn* must subordinate all order to process. Description of static elements is not enough to understand a
novel whose basis is change. Critics have tended to stress
the element of smoothness in the natural flow in *Huckleberry Finn*; thus Tony Tanner: "Through Huck Clemens
re-established a profoundly simple contact with a nature
whole and in process in all of its parts; the naïve vernacular child narrator provided him with a language which
could establish an effortless yet reverent rapport with the
empirical details of the seen flowing world, the world as
seen for the first time, that is." Tanner speaks of Huck's
craving for "even uninterrupted peace" in a world that is a
"continuous Sabbath."[3] This version of pastoral is a
natural corollary of the world seen as smooth flow, but I
must reject it along with other interpretations of the novel
as a hymn to nature, because such a view does not answer
the questions raised by the constant disordered activity,
the natural and human turbulence, of the novel. If the
characters cannot accept smoothness and order (as we
shall see), then the critic can hardly lay stress on it.

How does Twainian man experience his world? And
then, having established an attitude toward his world as a
result of his experience, what does he do? The answer
to my second question will take most of the rest of this
book and justify the controversial episodes of the novel.
The answer to the first question is simply that man in
Huckleberry Finn is a stranger in his world,[4] and his feelings
about that world are those of a stranger under stress—
uncertainty, anxiety, fear, even panic terror. Men reach

different solutions to the problems posed by nature and culture, which itself is a group of fossilized ad hoc solutions of former men to their own problems. The problems, however, are always the same, underneath the changing surface. It is difficult to see the problems clearly because Huck is not analytical; he habitually does not record details of behavior from which we could infer deep feelings, and in any case, some problems, like Tom Sawyer and Colonel Sherburn, are impervious to analysis. But we can feel the presence of the eternal problem of being strange; we can feel it in Pap, with his tirades and terrors, and we can feel it in Pap's son.

When Huck approaches the Phelps farm, hears the spinning wheel, and wishes he "was dead . . . and done with it all," he is defining "it" as his burden. Huck cannot explain, then or later, what he means by "it"; but at this point (chap. 32) a reader should know what "it" is— a cluster consisting of natural and cultural pressures, human anxieties resulting from those pressures, the endless efforts to relieve the anxieties, and the sense of futility arising from awareness of the failure or inadequacy of the efforts and the needlessness of the pressures. "It" is an existential matter, far beyond the social "coercion" defined as Huck's problem by some critics.[5] Rejection of the Rousseauistic idea of "coercion" of "the self" by "society" does not, however, mean abandoning the concept of the individual, or the possibility of the individual's being in conflict with his culture. As modern anthropology has shown, one may be well integrated into his culture and yet have a world-outlook of alienation. The culture in fact may be a vehicle for celebrating this outlook and at the same time trying to cope with it. This is the case in *Huckleberry Finn*.[6] In this novel all men are coerced by the human situation to coerce each other. The latter kind of coercion, the social kind, is what Huck calls "civilization" and flees from, but the former kind, the existential kind, is primary.

The pressure of the human situation, nature, is the cornerstone of *Huckleberry Finn*; everything is building upon it, although the building makes the cornerstone hard to see. This pressure gives nothing to man except the turbulence that he cannot bear. Man's sense of this pressure is instinctive and pre-verbal; his reaction to it is uncontrollable, though almost equally unconscious. Generally it is a constant pressure, best seen in the discussion of Bricksville, the grimmest town in the novel: "Such a town as that has to be always moving back, and back, and back, because the river's always gnawing at it" (chap. 21). When it comes to the pressure of nature, every town in the novel is "such a town as that," and every person a dweller in it. Twain himself dwelt in it and carried it around with him, so to speak, and his life was an "always moving," to which could be added, as he grew older, "back, and back, and back." This natural pressure creates the genuine religion of the novel, witchcraft, which unites master and slave in a community of anxiety (both Nat, the Phelpses' slave, and Huck tie up their hair with thread to keep the witches away). The belief in witches and ghosts provides as solid and artistically useful a religious basis for *Huckleberry Finn* as traditional Christianity does for the kind of novel admired by Henry James.[7]

Huck himself has many brushes with the pressure of nature, and two head-on confrontations with nature in its most frightening form—an endless, meaningless flux.

Because this formlessness challenges man's need for
organizing activity, Huck reacts against it violently and
revealingly. The two confrontations are placed strategically,
one at the beginning, and one at the moment of Huck's
arrival at the Phelps farm to rescue Jim.[8]

During the opening chapter Huck experiences the
pressures of "civilization" as harshly as he ever will.
"Miss Watson . . . had jist come to live with the Widow
Douglas," says Huck, giving the impression that Miss
Watson had been sent by some malignant agency to
harass him. Her nagging is ingenious. It combines bullying
with indifference, so that Huck is subject both to human
pressures ("She worked me middling hard for about an
hour") and natural ones ("Then for an hour it was deadly
dull, and I was fidgety"). Eventually she manages to
combine the two pressures: "Miss Watson she kept
pecking at me and it got tiresome and lonesome." When
Huck gets off by himself he is still in this mood, and,
being physically alone, passes into an ominous further
stage: "I felt so lonesome I most wished I was dead."
Then come wordless intimations of the particulars of
"death" (that is, raw nature) from the inhabitants and
familiars of that anti-world—owls, "whippowills," dogs, and
ghosts. "I got so downhearted and scared," Huck tells us.
"Scared," the primitive panic fear of nonhuman nature;
"downhearted," the despair at being in a world that can
do this to men and at feeling helpless to do anything about
it. And what does being downhearted and scared do to the
boy who a few minutes earlier could not wait to get off by
himself? "I did wish I had some company," he says, in a
striking demonstration of the dependence of man on
situation and of situation on natural pressure.

Huck's pipe helps to sustain him as the house becomes,

appropriately, "still as death," and the town clock strikes twelve—more than a banal melodramatic touch, midnight in this fictional world being the time when man has the least control over nature. In this situation it is appropriate for Huck to be grateful when he hears Tom Sawyer signaling for him. When seen against this background of pressure from nature, Huck's deep pleasure in the absurdities of Tom and his gang later that night makes sense, as the sign of his relief from the pressure.

The other confrontation, which is even more important, comes as Huck approaches the Phelps house full of dedication and enthusiasm for the rescue of Jim. It is high noon, another moment when time seems to stand still: "it was all still and Sunday-like" (chap. 32). There is no one around. In the air the "bugs and flies," aimless creatures, make "dronings," a word that well expresses a kind of activity that is worse to a human being than inactivity because its pointlessness and monotony deny the possibility of "meaningful" human activity, like static drowning out a radio frequency. These dronings are the kind "that makes it seem so lonesome and like everybody's dead and gone. . . ." "Lonesome" and "dead" describe conditioned responses that, as in the midnight scene, follow from the unbearable direct perception of inhuman, meaningless nature. After references again to breezes and spirits whispering, Huck concludes the opening paragraph of the chapter, "As a general thing it makes a body wish *he* was dead, too, and done with it all." At this stage in the discussion we can see better than before what "it" means (and at this stage in the reading of the novel, the little pronoun has the weight of thirty-one chapters behind it).

After a paragraph of stage-setting description of the

"little one-horse cotton plantation," Huck heads for the house and the climax of his experience: "When I got a little ways I heard the dim hum of a spinning-wheel wailing along up and sinking along down again; and then I knowed for certain I wished I was dead—for that *is* the lonesomest sound in the whole world." This sound was Twain's private symbol of the unbearable. In "The Private History of a Campaign That Failed," published less than two years after *Huckleberry Finn* was finished, Twain tells us of his company's stay at a farm:

> . . . After all these years the memory of the dullness, and stillness, and lifelessness of that slumberous farmhouse still oppresses my spirit with a sense of the presence of death and mourning. There was nothing to do, nothing to think about; there was no interest in life. . . . There was no sound but the plaintive wailing of a spinning-wheel, forever moaning out from some distant room,—the most lonesome sound in nature, a sound steeped and sodden with homesickness and the emptiness of life.[9]

This passage—quite the most rhetorical in this ironic essay —again offers the cluster of key words ("dullness," "stillness," "death," "lonesome"), and stresses the idea of man's need for activity, but ends with an explicitness that Huck is not capable of: "the emptiness of life." Life, in other words, is not occasionally empty; it is basically empty. One starts from emptiness and builds on it. Human culture, Twain realizes, is not "life," but an artificial creation made from it and sitting precariously atop it.

The connection of this sound with homesickness is confirmed by a passage dictated by Twain for his

autobiography in the late 1890s. Reminiscing about his
uncle John A. Quarles's farm near Florida, Missouri, he
said, "I can see the farm yet, with perfect clearness. I can
see all its belongings, all its details; the family room of
the house, with a trundle bed in one corner and a
spinning-wheel in another—a wheel whose rising and
falling wail, heard from a distance, was the mournfulest
of all sounds to me, and made me homesick and lowspirited,
and filled my atmosphere with the wandering spirits of
the dead."[10] In this chapter of classic American nostalgia
for childhood and the family farm, the symbol of life's
misery has a central place.

Responding so strongly to these terrible confrontations,
and describing them so vividly, Huck makes them stand
out from the other scenes of the novel; but although these
few situations differ in degree from most of the other
situations in which the characters find themselves, they do
not differ in kind. All situations in this novel demand and
receive response; human behavior, psychological or social,
is a function of situation. "Demand value" is the useful
term that social scientists use for this domination of
situation over response. A circular but clear definition is
Margaret Mead's: "The habit of taking each situation as
a single unit and adapting rapidly and fully to it . . . is
situational."[11] As a student of what people do rather than
what they ought to do or think they do, Twain might have
agreed with the statement of Jerome S. Bruner:
"Situations have a demand value that appears to have very
little to do with the motives that are operative. Surely
it isn't simply a 'motive to conform'; this is too great an
abstraction. . . . [Reciprocity] is about as primitive an
aspect of human behavior as we know." "Reciprocity,"

Taking these events on the level of the given turbulent world of flux and activity organized in immediate terms by the principle of situationalism, they are not only explicable but inevitable. In chapter 8 Huck sneers at "low-down cornpone" because he has just set his teeth into a loaf of "baker's bread," the food of the quality; but in chapter 17 he proclaims that "there ain't nothing better" than "cold corn-pone" because it helps satisfy his ravenous appetite in the security of the Grangerford house after the steamboat hits the raft and throws Huck into a terrifying crisis. During the fog episode (chap. 15) Huck is on the edge of panic but controls himself, because the situation demands a cool head if he is to survive and rejoin Jim. Huck allows his fear to emerge only in expressions like "I did wish the fool would think to beat a tinpan, and beat it all the time, but he never did." (Huck can be excused in this situation for not realizing that Jim cannot afford to attract attention.) Only after the emotional reunion with Jim can Huck afford to give full vent to his tension, by calling Jim "a tangle-headed old fool" and badgering him into the belief that the whole affair was a dream. Once Huck has discharged his feelings, he can apologize to Jim; and the two, all passion spent, can resume their quiet drifting. In chapter 3 Huck is still testing what "civilization" offers him, is under pressure from Miss Watson and Tom, and is about ready to chuck the whole thing, so he takes out his frustrations and boredom on the Sunday-school children without qualms and without any real malice —he is interested only in his own feelings.

In these and other episodes Huck acts on a principle that he can express only after writing about the greatest

says Bruner, "involves a deep human need to respond to others and to operate jointly with them toward an objective."[12]

The world of *Huckleberry Finn* is a situational world, and man in that world is situational man. The term "character," referring to a fixed structure of traits, is irrelevant and misleading; men are groups of potentialities that respond to situations. The "objective" toward which men "operate" is the organizing of situations into what I call dramas (see chapter 2), but that kind of responding, which often seems so voluntaristic and aggressive, is as helpless as passivity; consider Tom Sawyer in the hectic latter stages of the evasion (see below, pp. 178-79). A kind of temporary standoff, based on a response of fear and respect, is the best that man in this novel can hope to achieve, as Huck does in his idyllic moments.

Without using the term "demand value of situations," Twain thought in terms of the idea for most of his literary life. In the early 1870s, when he was beginning to turn toward his river material, Twain clearly saw man as a mechanism dominated by its situation and by the need to respond to, and become involved in, situations; see, for example, the marginal comments in Twain's copy of W. E. H. Lecky's *History of European Morals from Augustus to Charlemagne* (1869), discussed in Walter Blair's *Mark Twain and Huck Finn*.[13] By the time of *What Is Man?* Twain was setting forth the idea of situationalism with a belligerence that reveals his sincerity along with his amateurishness and his emotional desperation. "It isn't a philosophy, it is a fact," said Twain through his spokesman, the "Old Man," suggesting, along with the nervous truculence, that Twain was working from his own observations of mankind.[14] "The human being," says the Old Man, "is a chameleon; by the law of his nature he takes the color of his place of resort."[15] Eliminating Twain's overtones of contempt, we have here a satisfactory working definition of situational man. The mind, Twain further contends, not only responds to external stimuli but creates its own situations. A fifteen-minute reverie, says Twain's straight man, the "Young Man," is "a drifting panorama of ever-changing, ever-dissolving views manufactured by my mind without any help from me."[16] In *A Tramp Abroad* (1880), written during several of the years (1876–83) when Twain was erratically occupied with *Huckleberry Finn*, Twain used similar terms to suggest the dreamlike shifting vistas of an imaginary raft trip.[17] Twain spontaneously clothed his determinism in the kind of imagery from which *Huckleberry Finn* is constructed. As we shall see, river life and natural events such as sunrises are to Huck what the Young Man's reveries are to him, and in the novel man involuntarily "manufactures" artificial events, which I call "dramas," out of his situations, as the Young Man's mind "manufactures" its "panoramas."

In *What Is Man?* Twain's paired concepts, "temperament" and "training," the controlling influences on man's behavior along with situation, do not refer to immediate situations; but "training" does suggest the continuous situation of enculturation, the long process by which the infant is turned into a human being and a member of his culture, and a good deal of *Huckleberry Finn*, the beginning especially, is devoted to examining efforts to enculturate Huck. For the most powerful

revelation of Twain's realization of the demand value of situations, we can turn again to *What Is Man?*: man, "the chameleon, . . . has only to change his habitat —his *associations*. But the impulse to do it must come from the *outside*. . . . Sometimes a very small and accidental thing can furnish him the initiatory impulse and start him on a new road, with a new ideal."[18] In a late essay, "The Turning Point of My Life," in which Twain gave the final and strongest expression of his long obsession with the power of situation, he said, "Necessity is a *Circumstance*; Circumstance is man's master—and when Circumstance commands he must obey. . . . "[19] He went on to link "Circumstance" to "temperament," thus giving us for all practical purposes a modern deterministic psychological system to account for human behavior.

Thinking in terms of "situational man" trying to cope with the pressures of a turbulent world allows us to answer some perplexing questions, e.g., Why does Huck sneer at cornpone at one time but later say "there ain't nothing better"? Why does Huck, who is friendly and grateful to Jim most of the time, torment him after the fog episode? Why does Huck, the redemptive possibility of the human race, bully Sunday-school children? Why does Huck propose a practical plan to rescue Jim, and Tom an absurd plan? Why does Jim remain passive during the evasion but tell the Phelpses about the Royal Nonesuch? Why does Huck resolve to rescue Jim in chapter 31, but yield to Tom thereafter? Why does the Duke talk elegantly at one time, bluntly at another, coarsely at a third? Why does Jim call Huck "honey"?

immediate crisis of the novel, the denial of Jim's blackness to the slave-hunters (chap. 16). Huck realizes that his share of what Twain later called "training" is inadequate—"a body that don't get *started* right when he's little ain't got no show . . . there ain't nothing to back him up"—and concludes, "So I reckoned I wouldn't bother no more about it, but after this always do whichever come handiest at the time." "Whichever come handiest at the time"—that explains the situational Twain world. "Whichever" it is, it "come" by itself; that is, behavior is determined. It "come handiest": behavior obeys simple laws. It "come handiest at the time": behavior is special, temporal, without being consistent. The Huck of this philosophy seems very distant from the high-minded "saintly" Huck of Arnoldian criticism.

This key phrase, "whichever come handiest at the time," contrasts with another, "taking stock," which appears most often during Huck's gropings in the early chapters. To take stock in something is to make a commitment; it is to align oneself more or less permanently, according to an abstract principle. For Twain, with his complex feelings about money and making money, taking stock—speculating, as we would say—was tied up with his sense of personal worth (also a financial term in origin) and his personal identity. But during the 1890s Twain found out to his sorrow that in a real and changing world speculation was risky and that a man who identified himself with his speculations ran the risk of a loss greater than monetary loss, the loss of self-esteem. Jim learns this lesson when he "tackles stock" of a live kind, loses all his savings, and makes a fool of himself. Huck also learns that permanence and principles are irrelevant concepts in a situational world. Huck says, "I don't take no stock in dead people" (chap. 1), and he rejects a blanket commitment to the dead; but later he lectures Jim about medieval and biblical kings (chap. 14). Huck is not contradicting himself. The two episodes are governed by different principles. Interest in the dead has nothing to do with lecturing Jim about Solomon; a desire to impress Jim, to "show off," to display "style," has a great deal to do with it.

The traditional concepts of "comic character" and "tragic character" disappear along with the concept of character itself as the sum of fixed faculties and qualities. Instead, Twain shows us systems of potentials, ready to interact with situations in different ways, and driven to do so by the principle of reciprocity, with "comic" results in some cases and "tragic" ones in others. Character can still be evaluated, but only in situational terms. At the bottom are the loafers in Bricksville; at the top is Tom Sawyer. The loafers are Twain's control, his zero-mark, men in no situation, with no stimuli from nature and no help from their culture (which hardly exists anyway). We are shown in painful detail the actions of men in a non-situation: they cheat each other out of bits of tobacco and set fire to stray dogs. Huck is "better" than the loafers, not because he is inherently superior, but because he is luckier—he almost always has some opportunity for action, or is able to find action when he craves it (as he finds Jim or Mrs. Loftus or the King and the Duke). The chivying of the Sunday-school picnic shows what loutishness Huck is capable of when he is bored and lacking in chances for action. The example of

his father suggests what the wrong situation could
make Huck into.

Human behavior, however, does involve continuing
situations—the man-made ones, the dramas of culture,
which give some people more power than others.
Much of the novel depends on the continuing cultural
differences between Huck and Tom. Being part of a
favorable cultural situation—what Huck calls "the
quality"—Tom can ignore immediate situational demands
and give full rein to his vigorous temperament. In a
sense he must do that and do it all the time, for "the
quality," like any aristocracy, redefine and renew their
situation continually by showing that they can afford
to ignore the pressures that others must bow to. The
evasion is the great chance for Tom to demonstrate his
position on a large scale before a large audience; thus
Tom's passionate energy there, which alarms Huck
so much. Jim has nothing to do with it all, except to be
the occasion of the demonstration. For Tom, Jim's interest
in the evasion is "only personal," as Gatsby says of
Tom Buchanan's love for Daisy. The "authorities" and
the other nonsense in the ending have no point. That
is their point—to be "merely comic," as Henry Nash Smith
says; to be as far as possible from the grubby world
where actions must be tidy and sensible and consistent.
All this is behind Tom's startling attack on Huck's
plan of rescue: "What's the good of a plan that ain't
no more trouble than that?" (chap. 34). At the end comes
the nicest touch of all: while Huck, his situation suddenly
controlled by the suspicions of the adults, hunts for
some good lies to explain the evasion, Tom wakes up
and at once begins *to tell the truth* about the whole affair.

Only he can afford to. A few times circumstances—the
beginning of the *Walter Scott* episode, the return to the
raft after the fog—give Huck the feeling that he too can get
away with daring gestures of freedom, but he is quickly
taught his lesson each time: the river takes the raft
away from the wreck, Jim's anger makes Huck realize
that he needs Jim's friendship.

Jim is the most unlike Tom. Jim must be the most
fully alert to situations, and is the most bound and
victimized by them, for by cultural definition he is a
passive victim in a permanent situation, slavery. Jim and
the other slaves are the most alert and cunning of the
characters. In the course of this bloody, death-haunted
novel not one black person dies. Many of the whites
go too far, do stupid things for no visibly necessary reason,
and are destroyed; the slaves never "go" at all, except
under the most pressing or the most favorable conditions.
Pressed by Miss Watson's threat to sell him into slow
but certain death down the river, Jim reacts instantly and
strongly, and with a craft worthy of Huck or Tom at
his best. Bullied and sold by the King and the Duke, Jim
does nothing in revenge until the one perfect opportunity
presents itself: he learns that the two rascals are going
to put on the Royal Nonesuch again. Then he acts.
He tells the Phelpses "all about that scandalous show"
(chap. 33). The King and the Duke die, horribly. Jim
is perfectly secure in his revenge; he is upheld, in fact, by
all of the outraged Puritanism of the culture. Huck,
predictably, fails to see that the event is Jim's revenge.

The great reverie, in chapter 31, in which Huck vows
to steal Jim despite the mores of his culture, arises
from Huck's circumstances and depends throughout on

them, along with his "training," the residue of earlier
situations. This, after all, is what a reverie is—the
presentation of the flux of the mind itself, a series of
mental situations that result from earlier ones and cause
later ones. Huck's sense of shame arises partly from
the addition of his training to the neutral statement, based
on Huck's knowledge, that "it would get all around that
Huck Finn helped a nigger to get his freedom." The
chiding voice—"the plain hand of Providence" that watches
"all the time from up there in heaven"—is the voice of
Miss Watson. Earlier Huck rejected her; now he
accepts her. Huck has not changed, but his situation
has, and the Watson ethos and manner now mesh with
it. Huck's shame also comes by a process of association
from the beginning of the reverie. It is sad, Huck thinks,
that Jim is now a slave again; it would be better if
he were a slave at home; a letter home would fix that
up; it would work to Jim's disadvantage, because
Miss Watson would despise Jim for being ungrateful;
everybody despises an ungrateful slave; everybody
despises a nigger-stealer; Huck is a nigger-stealer. The
pressure on Jim would itself be a situation—"they'd make
Jim feel it all the time." Jim's "rascality and ungratefulness
for leaving her" are taken for granted. In the large
situation of Huck's culture a slave who runs off is an
ungrateful rascal. Huck has never questioned that general
rule or the foundation of his culture in slavery. He has
questioned religion, so the elements of religious "training"
enter later, after Huck has built up a load of guilt and
has allowed the situation to simmer ("the more I studied
about it . . ."). Here Twain illustrates the general
principle that the demand value of situations depends

on the sum of many factors in the present and from the past.

The ending, the aftermath of Huck's reverie, is the novel's clinching demonstration of situationalism. The ending is a disaster, most people feel, and only a sadist or a child can get unalloyed pleasure out of it; but the disaster is inevitable. Huck cannot help letting his conscious commitment to rescue Jim take a back seat to Tom and his antics. We are in a world where conscious commitments are secondary to the governing forces, to what Twain later called "the Master": "It is as I have said: the thing which will give you the *most* pleasure, the most satisfaction, in any moment or *fraction* of a moment, is the thing you will always do. You must content the Master's *latest* whim, whatever it may be."[20] In such a world it is indeed ominous to see Huck slowly approaching the Phelps house and "not fixing up any particular plan, but jist trusting to Providence to put the right words in my mouth when the time come" (chap. 32). Huck's "Providence" amounts to the "demand value" of situations, and his trust is a form of capitulation to this governing power, capped by his justification for that trust: "I'd noticed that Providence always did put the right words in my mouth if I left it alone" (chap. 32). This amounts to saying, "Whatever is, is right," or, as we have seen Huck putting it, "I reckoned I wouldn't bother no more about it, but after this always do whichever come handiest at the time." In the situational world of *Huckleberry Finn* this philosophy is hopelessly weak. It happens that Huck's comment about doing "whichever come handiest" follows his instinctive and (to the reader) wholly admirable defense

of Jim from the slave-hunters (chap. 16), so the broad
inapplicability of the general philosophy is concealed in
the acceptability of the particular example. Or, to put it
another way, if we accept the philosophy of "whichever
come handiest" in chapter 16, then we must accept it
in the ending too; and then we must accept the ending.

When one considers the language of the novel in terms
of situationalism, it falls into a new pattern, as the
plot does. Henry Nash Smith has acutely observed
that the language of *Huckleberry Finn* is two languages,
a "vernacular," the unselfconscious colloquial
American speech, and an "official" language, a
self-conscious system designed for making impressions
and expressing overt values. This approach, good as
taxonomy, is inadequate in terms of the dynamics of the
novel. In these terms we have an Emersonian situation,
Man Talking, a dynamic linguistic unity in which
the momentary sum of situational factors, "temperament,"
and "training" dictates the choice of words. ("Training,"
of course, is a product of past situations; "temperament,"
like situations, is a given.) If we postulate, as Professor
Smith does not, a consistently superior "vernacular"
language and a consistently inferior "official" language,
then it is hard to deal with the fact that the superior
language is spoken by the worst characters in the
book as well as the best—if Huck is the best—and the
inferior language is spoken by some of the better
characters. Professor Smith points out the fact; I think
that we can go a step further and explain it if we drop
the rigid linguistic categories, except as identifying
tags, and see language as a unity from which choices are
made by situation.

24

The Bricksville loafers are again the zero-markers,
victims of entropy. In the absence of personal skills
and outside pressures beyond the need to kill time, they
drift to the bottom of language considered as a medium for
social interaction. The loafers' speech is undeniably
vernacular. So is the King's, when he is not trying
to make an impression. "What are you heaving your
pore broken heart at *us* f'r?" he snarls at the Duke, when
the latter is preparing to make himself top rascal on
the raft by cleverly using sententious rhetoric, impressive
and thus appropriate to the situation. The slow-witted
King finally catches on and clumsily mouths enough
appropriate bilge to supersede the Duke. But training
and temperament, or rather the lack of them, finally
catches up with the King in later linguistic situations.
When he talks to the prayer meeting at Pokeville, his
linguistic limitations are concealed by his narrative skill
and by the situation (the ignorance of the crowd and
their hysterical craving for any kind of stimulus). At
the Wilkses the King is finally defeated by his inability
to step fully beyond the vernacular. He makes the error
of casting the Duke, the better non-vernacular talker of the
pair, as the deaf-and-dumb brother. The expert
imitation of a minister that the situation demands cannot
be furnished by the King, whose desperate efforts merely
make him look like a fool to Huck and to the handful
of townspeople whose temperaments allow them to see the
King as he is rather than in terms of their own desires.
Ironically, the King's final downfall has nothing to do
with language; he never has a chance to speak before the
mob seizes him (chap. 33).

Huck's own language and the effects of its use are

likewise influenced by the shifting equations of situation.
The book itself is a giant situation, or rather the writing
of it is. The narrative passages of the novel are more
precise and expressive than the reported dialogue;
the narrative has been made, it is artificial, a product
of effort. Huck is fully aware of all this. At the end he
says, "If I'd a knowed what a trouble it was to make a
book I wouldn't a tackled it, and ain't agoing to no
more." The strong colloquial flavor of the passage, and the
"bad" grammar and numerous contractions, reflect
a kind of ostentatious falling-off of effort, like the
handwriting of a student rushing through the last sentences
of an impromptu essay. Many of the narrative and
descriptive passages are written with care, and it is from
these passages that one derives the sense of the greatness of
the "vernacular" prose style. But the "vernacular
style" is not colloquial. As Huck makes clear in his rueful
remark, his prose is literary, written—thought up,
thought over, and put down on paper. (I will return to
this important point below, pp. 115-16.) To sweep every
sloppy colloquial utterance in the novel into one
classification with Huck's great descriptive and narrative
passages is to repeat in reverse the error of the Concord
librarians who banned the entire book as vulgar.

Huck's own speech also varies according to the
situation, but since he lacks facility in the immediate use
of words, the variations are few and awkward. When
lecturing Jim on kings and the Bible, Huck talks like a
mediocre Tom Sawyer, an imitation of an imitation.
Tom uses his pedantic prattle for the sound reason
that it helps him attain and keep power over his world.
But Huck can dazzle only Jim, who by the harsh cultural

definition is of no importance. Given the laws of drama, the human need to organize and to display organizing power, and the situation—for some time Jim is Huck's only audience—Huck has no choice but to try to impress him, but that does not change the triviality of the material and the situation. Huck has little motivation or opportunity to use cant skillfully and sustainedly, and most of the time he does not use it at all. In speech he drifts into the ordinary colloquial style of his time and place. Only in the leisured situation of writing after the evasion does Huck find the outlet for his energies, in the carefully wrought narrative style and the thoughtful comments on men and events. The book itself is thus the domain of Huck's verbal efforts, and his audience is the invisible reader.

Huck makes extensive use of conventional "literary" language only in his great reverie (chap. 31), where the fear of public opinion modulates into the voice of conscience speaking in Miss Watson's style of evangelical Protestantism—"the plain hand of Providence," "there's one that's always on the lookout," and so on. As mimesis this is excellent; as logical fiction it is dubious (see below, pp. 143-48). Fortunately, the earlier part of the reverie is completely logical in cultural terms; in a monolithic slave culture Huck did not need to go to Sunday school to learn that helping Jim is shameful. This section of the reverie follows from the thoughts about how "ornery and disgraced" Jim would feel if caught. Twain's masterstroke here is to show us unobtrusively how the pressures of situation and "training" can make an "ungrateful nigger," even one with Jim's free temperament, agree with his tormentors. The language is genuine vernacular:

And then think of *me*! It would get all around, that Huck
Finn helped a nigger to get his freedom; and if I was ever to
see anybody from that town again, I'd be ready to get down
and lick his boots for shame. That's just the way: a person
does a low-down thing, and then he don't want to take no consequences of it. Thinks as long as he can hide it, it ain't no
disgrace. That was my fix exactly.

Up to this point the sequence is flawless. The shame arises
from "training," the general comments from personal
experience. The comments—"as long as he can hide it,
it ain't no disgrace"—are a devastating statement of
the rotting Puritanism of Huck's culture; all he needs
to add in order to sum up his world is something like
"And if he can't hide it, then it still ain't no disgrace as
long as he can make himself and others think it's not a
low-down thing." But after this sequence Huck starts
talking about conscience, and the motive of the scene
shifts from Huck's to Twain's own concerns. I think,
therefore, that an argument about the opposition
of "vernacular" and "official" language should find a
better example than this scene.

Another example of the language of the novel can
be studied situationally. This is Jim's use of "honey"
and "chile" in addressing Huck. In the well-known
article "Come Back to the Raft Agin, Huck, Honey,"
Leslie Fiedler bases on this usage much of his influential
claim that Huck and Jim are consciously or unconsciously
homosexuals and thus illustrative of a far-reaching
tendency in American culture.[21] Considering the
social significance of these epithets, one can only say
that, as Fiedler apparently did not know, they were and
are common southern forms of address from adults to
children (though not from white adults to black children),

and that the overtones of the two words are not always
affectionate, sometimes quite the opposite, especially in
the case of "child." Within *Huckleberry Finn* the two
words have these situational meanings; in fact, the matter
is such a locus classicus of the dominance of situation
in this novel that it is worth some close reading.

Huck is called "honey" and "chile" by two characters,
Jim and Mrs. Loftus. Mrs. Loftus and Huck can hardly
be linked in any kind of sexual relationship. In
accordance with the value of the words in the southern
vocabulary, this peppery woman calls Huck "honey"
when she still thinks that he is a girl, and "child"
when she learns, to her satisfaction, that he is a boy. Jim
and Mrs. Loftus are the only lower-class characters
who are nice to Huck; some of the quality are, but they are
too distant to address him as "honey" or "child." The
kindly feelings of Jim and Mrs. Loftus take special form,
depending on their own situations, when they are directed
toward a child rather than an adult. Two of Jim's uses
of "honey" and one of "chile," as well as Mrs. Loftus's
two uses of "honey," are patronizing and superior.
Beginning to realize that "Sarah Williams" is not all
she says she is, Mrs. Loftus says, "What did you say
your name was, honey?" On being told that the name is
"Mary Williams," Mrs. Loftus continues, "Honey, I
thought you said it was Sarah when you first come in?"
She is being sly, not affectionate. After she has forced
Huck out of his pose and is feeling rather pleased with
herself (so that she cannot see through his new pose),
she patronizingly calls him "child": "Goshen, child?
This ain't Goshen." Whether she is saying "honey"
or "child" her attitude is always superior, and not at all
affectionate.

Jim's suggestions of superiority all come early in his life with Huck, while they are isolated on Jackson's Island. Here and only here is it possible for Jim to be superior; on the river and elsewhere he is too dependent on Huck. When Huck remarks that it is nice to be in a cave out of the rain and the flood-water, Jim replies triumphantly: "Well, you wouldn't a ben here, 'f it hadn't a ben for Jim. Wou'd a ben down dah in de woods widout any dinner, en gittin' mos' drowned, too, dat you would, honey. Chickens knows when it's gwyne to rain, en so do de birds, chile" (chap. 9). The adult as initiate and expert, the child as naïve ignoramus: the cultural role is there for the taking, and Jim plays it to the hilt. It is hard to see here any sexual application, overt or latent. A little later, when Huck says that the loot from the floating house shows the error in the snakeskin superstition, Jim replies, "Never you mind, honey, never you mind. Don't you get too peart. It's a-comin'. Mind I tell you, it's a-comin' " (chap. 10). Of course Jim is right; the two often have trouble, usually because Huck is "peart." To the role of superior adult watching over the heedless child, Jim adds that of the knower of mysteries instructing the layman. Faulkner has a similar usage in the first part of *The Sound and the Fury*:

> *How will they know it's Dilsey, when it's long forgot, Dilsey, Caddy said.*
> *It'll be in the Book, honey, Dilsey said. Writ out.*

Later, when the situation forces a reversal of roles, Jim's use of "honey" and "chile" is full of blind gratitude. The various crises—the encounter with the slave-hunters, the betrayal of the King—make the point of role-reversal explicit; they put Jim in situations so terrible that

just surviving them leaves him broken down. When Huck
and Tom enter Jim's cabin at the Phelpses, after he has
been an isolated prisoner for a day or so, "he was so
glad to see us he most cried; and called us honey, and
all the pet names he could think of" (chap. 36). This is
not sex; it is pathetic joy at the sight of friends and the
hope of rescue. To link sex with the use of "honey" here is
an insult to Jim and his situation as a prisoner,
a black man, and a slave. The matter of real interest
here is Huck's failure to realize Jim's position. He
reports Jim's rapture without comment, just as he merely
reports Jim's agreement, a little later, with Tom's plan
to put off the escape until they have had some fun—as if
Jim had any alternative!

The same pathetic joy is found elsewhere. When
Huck finds the raft again after the fog, Jim says, "You's
back ag'in? It's too good for true, honey, it's too good for
true. Lemme look at you, chile, lemme feel o' you. No,
you ain' dead! . . . thanks to goodness!" (chap. 15).
"Thanks to goodness," to be sure. Without Huck, Jim
is a lone black man, obviously a runaway slave, on a
raft in the middle of the Mississippi, with a slave state on
one side and a slave state (Kentucky) or a hostile free
state (southern Illinois) on the other. "Feeling of"
Huck is not sexual. It is necessary, given the witchcraft-
religion of the novel, because a person ostensibly
returned alive from a dangerous experience may actually
be his ghost returned to haunt you. Tom Sawyer feels
Huck, at Huck's suggestion, when Tom encounters
what he is sure is Huck's ghost on the road near the
Phelpses, hundreds of miles from where Huck "died."

Shortly after the fog episode, Jim's position changes

only to get worse. While Huck is enjoying himself at
the Grangerfords, Jim is immobilized in the depths of
the swamp. Huck does not grasp the overtones of this
situation when he encounters it; he visits Jim and leaves
him again. Jim's rapturous greeting here ("He nearly
cried, he was so surprised") has no more effect on
Huck than Nat's rapturous thanks ("Will you do it,
honey?—will you? I'll wusshup de groun' und' you' foot,
I will!") have on Tom after Tom promises to make a
witch pie for Nat (chap. 36). Jim does use "honey"
once in the Grangerford scene, at the close when he
comments on the Grangerford slaves: "Dey's mighty
good to me, dese niggers is, en whatever I wants 'm
to do fur me, I doan' have to ast 'm twice, honey"
(chap. 18). The word here is the product of Jim's
expansiveness in his new mood of relative security and
confidence.

Jim does not stick to "honey" and "chile" (not that
he uses those words much). When he is arguing with Huck
man to man, which in the world of this novel means
"enslaved black man to free white man," Jim uses the
word "boss": "Well, looky here, boss, dey's sumfn wrong,
dey is" (chap. 15). The term, half servile and half
aggressive, is nicely fitted to the particular situation and
to the general culture, a culture of slavery. Situation
is everything, and situations change. These two postulates
of this novel are again revealed here.

II

Thus each character responds to the demand value of
each situation. The movement of the novel from situation

to situation depends also on underlying levels of laws
or "structure" of which the characters, including Huck,
are not aware, even if they manipulate situations skillfully.
In obeying the law of demand value of situations,
Twain's characters bring the structural rules into action,
producing further situations that in turn demand
actions and reactions that in turn create further situations,
and so on. The characters move geographically in a
roughly straight line from Missouri to lower Arkansas;
culturally they move along a line of increasing intensity
of the great cultural factor, slavery. Neither factor
satisfactorily explains the movement from one incident
to another. On the surface the incidents have no
connection, so that many critics have seen the novel as a
picaresque fiction held together only by the personality
of its narrator. But on the level of deep structure the
episodes are related, in terms of the emotional state that
leads Huck (or Huck and another character) into the
incident or causes him to leave it. The movement of
emotional states is circular, although the sequence is
often broken or distorted by situations or the interference
of another character. The basic sequence, picking a
point of entry arbitrarily, is (1) peace and passivity,
(2) boredom and yearning for action, (3) excitement in
action and in involvement with others, (4) irritation at
troubles and dangers arising from action, (5) nervousness
or fear in flight that leads to security and inaction and
thus to peace. The greater (usually in intensity) one
stage, the greater the next. Thus *Huckleberry Finn*
satisfies Jean Piaget's dictum that "the notion of
structure is comprised of three key ideas: the idea of
wholeness, the idea of transformation, and the idea of
self-regulation."[22]

Differences in intensity can be deceiving in this novel.
One of the stages may be inconspicuous or completely
implied, but that is a characteristic of deep structure
and makes no difference. When Huck goes from the
idyllic peace of the raft (in chap. 19) to the raucous
involvement of the episodes with the King and the Duke
(chaps. 19-31), he seems to skip the stage of boredom,
and he apparently does not seek action or involvement. But
when Huck encounters the two rascals in the woods
(chap. 19), he abandons the idyll without a thought,
helps the pair willingly, and soon becomes involved in
their world despite his strong objections to them. If Huck
were not ready to move on from the inaction and peace
of the idyll, he would continue to act as circumspectly
as he does during the idyll (hiding during the day, and so
on) or he would escape from the rascals during one of
his several chances to do so (at the camp meeting,
during the Sherburn uproar and the Nonesuch
performances, and so on). At times, as in the sequence
after Huck's escape from Pap's cabin, the categories
are so conspicuous that even Huck is vaguely aware of
them, though he cannot realize that one emotional state is
the consequence of the other. In a few of his most
intense experiences Huck can see connections. He realizes
that the involvement with the Grangerfords led to
trouble, and several months later he is still wishing that he
had not "ever come ashore . . . to see such things"
(chap. 18).

Intensity also has internal structural effects satisfying
the requirement of self-regulation, that is, that a change
in the system must lead to another change that leads
to a new harmony. In Pap's cabin Huck is close to death;
his subsequent escape is therefore complex and intense in

mood, his sense of peace on the river and Jackson's
Island total, and his subsequent boredom, action
(roaming the island), and involvement with Jim equally
great and portentous. The overwhelming catastrophe
of the Grangerford episode produces an equivalent peace
on the raft ("Two or three days . . . swum by"). Huck's
sense of time changes so that these "two or three days"
seem much longer to him and to us—so much longer to
many readers, in fact, that from this brief episode has
largely grown the widespread sense of the raft voyage as
a timeless idyll. In contrast the Wilks episode seems
long to most readers and interminable to Huck, partly
for the reason that he has been with the King and the
Duke for a long time and is bored and exasperated
with them. Earlier, just an hour or so with Miss Watson
drives Huck into the depths of misery because she
puts so much pressure on him. Boredom can be staved
off or decreased by a succession of diverting man-made
events, as in the opening chapters (the robber gang,
trying prayer), or in the rich variety of the King-and-Duke
episode, or by a string of interesting but not frightening
natural events, as in the weeks Jim and Huck spend
watching storms and floods on Jackson's Island. But
the staved-off boredom always comes, leading in the cases
mentioned to hasty strong actions by Huck—his clumsy
involvement in the Wilks business and his nearly
disastrous journey in girl's clothes to Mrs. Loftus—or
to grateful acquiescence in actions of others ("It was
kind of lazy and jolly, laying off comfortable all day"
in Pap's cabin).

Overriding the passively endured situational sequence
is the actively created dramatic episode, and because it

can dominate and break up the round of the emotional
structure, for a time at any rate, I will take up this
crucial kind of sequence later in isolation and detail.
There are other key structural situations to be examined
here: the paradigmatic escape from Pap's cabin and
the controversial ending.

After getting away from Pap, Huck achieves a
momentary stability through the exhaustion of conflicting
impulses after prolonged conflict. Since the beginning
of the novel he has been in conflict with nature, Miss
Watson, Tom Sawyer, and Pap. He has bested Pap,
Miss Watson, and Tom in turn, by escaping from the
cabin, by making it look as if he were dead, and by doing
the whole thing with "style." Completely at peace, and
close to the fundamentals of nature—"everything was
dead quiet, and it looked late, and *smelt* late"—Huck
yields himself to the now-pleasant flow of nature: "I
got out amongst the driftwood, and then laid down in the
bottom of the canoe and let her float. I laid there, and
had a good rest and a smoke out of my pipe, looking
away into the sky; not a cloud in it. The sky looks ever so
deep when you lay down on your back in the moonshine;
I never knowed it before." Twain is nodding here, for
Huck has seldom slept under a roof and ought to
know the effects of moonlight. At any rate, one expects
a long and thorough communion with nature, especially
if one sees Huck as a pastoral hero. But the Emersonian
yielding to the perfect whole ends there; we are not in
the world of the Transcendentalists, and we are not
dealing with a conscious mystic. The world of man
intrudes: "And how far a body can hear on the water
such nights! I heard people talking at the ferry-landing. I

heard what they said, too—every word of it." Does Huck
resent this interruption? No, he enjoys it at the time;
he listens to what the people at the landing are saying
until he drifts downstream and can hear then no more.
Several months later, he accepts the interruption
again, this time by recording it carefully on paper.

Shortly after hearing the men, he is again in nature as
he lands on Jackson's Island and looks out "on the
big river and the black driftwood and way over to the
town, three mile away." He is in nature ("the big river"),
but still in relation to man ("the town"). Again he
turns to the man-made world as he tells us how he
watches a lumber raft float past and hears men giving
commands on it. This example is more delicate than the
first, in which there is a harsh contrast between the
fathomless moonlight and the raucous jesters at the ferry
landing. Here the human, the lumber raft, is integrated
into nature, floating with the current, as Huck was
earlier, and the commands of the raftsmen are in
harmony with the situation. With man and nature in
harmony, for the time being, it is possible for Huck to
go to sleep and wake up the next morning "feeling rested
and ruther comfortable and satisfied" (chap. 8).

Huck's world is never more harmonious than this, and
the satisfied feeling lasts for a record time, "three days
and nights. No difference—just the same thing." But
Huck can stand no more of this peaceful inaction, even
though he sits on the bank and counts "stars and
drift-logs and rafts" in order to defeat his loneliness and
boredom. He destroys the situation deliberately by
exploring the island, "mainly," he says, "in order to put
in the time." This desire to kill time and escape the

static, even if the static is idyllic, leads to the meeting and involvement with Jim and thus the action of the last three-quarters of the novel.

No other reaction from nature is as marked as this one, excepting, of course, the two moments of panic when Huck is in his room (chap. 1) and when he arrives at the Phelpses (chap. 32). Huck's last two major reactions in the novel, the ones leading to the final episode and away from it, are against social involvements (with the two rascals and the Phelps world) rather than against nature. The sequence leading to the evasion has complications that contribute to the unsatisfactory qualities of the evasion itself. After Huck revolts against the King and the Duke, he returns to the solitude of the raft, where he enters not nature but a state of nature in which it is possible for this white boy to dedicate himself to the service of a black slave. In this exalted, open, and vulnerable mood Huck approaches the Phelps house only to be confronted with the terrific blankness of nature at its most pure and least human. The experience leaves Huck shattered. Presented a few minutes later with the chance to reenter structured human life as Tom Sawyer, a leading symbol of the world rejected in chapter 31, Huck unhesitatingly chooses the organized acceptable lie and repudiates the disorganized unbearable truth. Huck's decision makes it impossible to help Jim on the level of dedication and sacrifice that Huck reached so painfully in chapter 31, and makes it possible for the rescue to be the perversion that Tom Sawyer makes it.

In the last pages of the novel Huck again reacts against "civilization," but thanks to the satisfactions of

his recent experiences as and with Tom Sawyer, the
reaction is much less violent and complete than
the one in chapter 32. Still ready for a limited kind
of involvement, Huck falls in easily with Tom's plan to
continue their antics in the Indian Territory. A few
paragraphs later, Huck announces that he has decided to
leave ahead of the rest, not in order to get away from
them but to counter Aunt Sally's scheme to "sivilize"
him. There is no sharp anxiety here, nor is there
anticipation of delight and rest in nature. Huck may
remember those idyllic moments on the river—in fact, he
just got through writing about them—but he cannot
link memory to anticipation because that would require
a coherent world, and he lives in a world of changing
situations that he experiences as changing pressures and
changing emotional responses to them. The only anticipation
he has and can have is that something will turn up that
he can turn into diversion. He does not set nature against
civilization in general; he sets his own cycles of activities
against the demands of the cycles of others.

It is a sign of Tom Sawyer's genius that he can use
Huck as an instrument and at the same time make
Huck feel that he is a friend and a collaborator—a naïve
and slow-witted collaborator, but one just the same
(see below, pp. 172-76). Other characters in the novel are
not so clever, and with them Huck passes rapidly through
the stages of involvement, irritation, and flight. Miss
Watson bluntly, and the Widow Douglas gently, try to ram
their styles down Huck's throat. It takes Huck only a
few moments to see through and reject them. Huck
turns to Tom's gang and accepts it until the assault on the
Sunday-school picnic destroys the illusion that the

gang is his gang as well as Tom's. Huck avoids Tom
thereafter until the very different situation of the ending.
Living at Pap's cabin is pleasant for Huck until Pap
casts him as the victim in a paranoid fantasy. The
Grangerfords too are delightful until Huck becomes an
unwitting instrument in their highly organized
"civilization," the feud. The Grangerfords' world is
so fully integrated and isolated that in the crisis Buck
assumes that Huck is a skilled feuder and depends on
him to keep close watch on the Shepherdsons. Buck
was wrong, but Huck never does realize it.

With the King and the Duke, Huck goes through a
similar but longer sequence of relationships. At first,
on the raft, Huck is the spectator, amused, aware that the
men are frauds, but unaware that he might become
unpleasantly involved with them. At Pokeville camp
meeting Huck is still the pure spectator; at Bricksville
he becomes a minor collaborator, helping with "our show"
and enjoying the Nonesuch swindle. At the Wilkses,
however, Huck is forced to play an active, demanding
part. His clumsiness with the "harelip" (Joanna Wilks)
reveals his unwillingness to obey the con men. It is
not entirely a question of skill; Huck handles more
delicate situations capably in earlier episodes. When his
anger at the King and the Duke passes a crucial point,
Huck is provoked into a complex counter-scheme
that he handles fairly well until he is upset by the ultimate
kind of pressure—brute force, in the shape of "that big
husky Hines" (chap. 29), who drags Huck off to the
cemetery and almost to his death.

The most subtle and important revelations of the effects
of pressure are visible in the relation of Huck and

Jim. Here there is involvement that does not arise from
overt aggressiveness or superior finesse, but from a
claim made in the name of friendship. Before Jim
says why he is on Jackson's Island, he makes sure of
Huck:

> " . . . You wouldn't tell on me ef I 'uz to tell you, would
> you, Huck?"
> "Blamed if I would, Jim."
> "Well, I b'lieve you, Huck. I—I *run off.*"
> "Jim!"
> "But mind, you said you wouldn't tell—you know you said
> you wouldn't tell, Huck."
> "Well, I did. I said I wouldn't, and I'll stick to it. Honest
> *injun*, I will. People would call me a low-down Abolitionist
> and despise me for keeping mum—but that don't make no
> difference. I ain't a-going back there anyways." (Chap. 8)

This is Huck's moment of commitment to Jim, a much
more important moment than the celebrated "I'll go to
hell" speech of chapter 31, where Huck merely
reconfirms what he says here (and confirms again in
the encounter with the slave-hunters in chapter 16).
To make Huck his instrument, Jim takes advantage
of a conditioned response, the boys' ethic that one should
not "tell." This is an artificial ethic, a dramatic
construction including friendship but transcending it, and
in the immediate situation even transcending the
most powerful organizing concept in this culture, the idea
of slavery. Twain is cheating here: he is bringing
some qualities of the boys' world of *The Adventures of
Tom Sawyer* into a very different world that is connected
to the earlier quite tenuously by the brief references to
Twain and Tom Sawyer in the opening paragraphs

of *Huckleberry Finn*. At any rate, although Twain makes
the claims of boys' honor irresistible to Huck, it is
clear, when Huck refers to what people might say, that he
feels at once the difficulty, the pressure, of his situation.
Huck goes on to defy public opinion, and gives two
reasons for his defiance—his vow and, as a casual
afterthought, the fact that he "ain't a-going back there
anyways."

In that phrase is the seed of Huck's later shameful
relations with Jim. At the time the point is comforting
to the characters and the reader. If Huck is not going back,
what difference does it make what St. Petersburg thinks
of him? But, given the Twain principle of activity,
Huck is sure to go somewhere, just to be going, and
given the actual situation—the river, Huck's weakness,
Jim's helplessness—it is likely that their movement
will involve drifting in more ways than one. Huck is not
going "back there," but he *is* going down the river, into
the Deep South, to settings that make "back there" look
peaceful.

Huck has no sense of the implications of his involvement
and his comments, and indeed never understands why
he treats Jim the way he does, with alternate affection
and indifference. Huck does accept the pressure that Jim
has put upon him by binding him to the boys' code of
honor. Huck keeps his word—he never tells on Jim,
and he does help him. But all this "pulls tight" on Huck,
as he would say, and he makes Jim pay and pay for
it. Huck puts the snakeskin in Jim's bed, conveniently
forgetting the probable consequences; Huck forces Jim
onto the *Walter Scott*; Huck makes Jim miserable
after the fog because Huck was miserable during it;

Huck forgets Jim during the Grangerford episode; Huck
condones the Duke's cruel treatment of Jim; Huck
allows Tom Sawyer to treat Jim as a plaything during the
ending. Over all is the raft's endless southward drift,
generating the tensions of the relationship out of the
flux of nature. When Huck fails to spot the junction of the
Ohio and the Mississippi, he is punishing Jim, and
also punishing himself for being a "low-down Abolitionist."
Jim cannot complain. His strategy of appealing to Huck's
dramatic sense does succeed; Huck does keep his word,
even when he does not want to, in chapter 16 when he
faces the slave-hunters. Only when Huck drives Jim to
the limit does Jim complain, as in the quarrel after the
fog, and even those objections depend largely on the
situation. Jim does not and cannot object to Huck's neglect
at the Grangerfords and later.

The pressure of this relationship is increased by the
closed nature of the world of the novel. A unified
world is a closed world. Huck therefore cannot escape
Jim because there is no escape. Huck and Jim cannot
go North, up the Ohio, because there is no North; it is
just a fantasy that people talk and dream about, like Moscow
for Chekhov's three sisters. "North" is a fantasy of
agreeable, sensible organization; "South," where the
characters find themselves imprisoned, is the real world
of turbulence and drift and man's clumsy scramble to
control or to escape from them. Huck and Jim must
go into the Deep South, the heart of pressure from nature
and man—or rather, the raft must take them there—
because we are in a determined world, not a voluntaristic
world. We are a long way from the glorious, fresh, open
world postulated for this novel by Tony Tanner (*The
Realm of Wonder*) and Bernard De Voto.

1. "The Genteel Tradition in American Philosophy," in Douglas L. Wilson, ed., *The Genteel Tradition: Nine Essays by George Santayana* (Cambridge, Mass.: Harvard University Press, 1967), p. 51. Leo Marx uses Santayana's remark to help establish Twain's failure (see "Mr. Eliot, Mr. Trilling, and *Huckleberry Finn*," p. 432).

2. Laura Thompson, *Toward a Science of Mankind* (New York: McGraw-Hill, 1961), pp. 88—89.

3. Tony Tanner, *The Realm of Wonder: Naivety and Reality in American Literature* (Cambridge: At the University Press, 1965), pp. 125, 162—63.

4. The consensus of modern Twain criticism is that the archetypal Twain character, from "The Jumping Frog" to the late manuscript fragments, is the stranger. The "transcendent" man, a type of Satanic stranger beginning with Colonel Sherburn, is discussed in *Mark Twain: The Development of a Writer*, p. 136. See also Lynn, *Mark Twain and Southwestern Humor*, pp. 246—47. For the late manuscripts see William M. Gibson, ed., *Mark Twain's "Mysterious Stranger" Manuscripts* (Berkeley and Los Angeles: University of California Press, 1969), pp. 1—34.

5. E.g., *Mark Twain: The Development of a Writer*, pp. 122—23; Lionel Trilling, Introduction to *The Adventures of Huckleberry Finn* (rpt. New York: Rinehart, 1948), p. vi.

6. A parallel is the paranoid Dobu culture discussed in Ruth Benedict's classic *Patterns of Culture* (rpt. Boston: Houghton Mifflin, 1959), pp. 130—72.

7. Bernard De Voto discusses the meaning and functions of witchcraft in the novel in *Mark Twain's America*, pp. 66—67.

8. The first and still the most important discussion of these passages and of Twain's obsession with spinning wheels is in *Mark Twain: The Development of a Writer*, pp. 130—31. Professor Smith is mainly concerned to demonstrate Twain's free-floating guilt; my approach to, and use of, these passages is quite different.

9. "The Private History of a Campaign That Failed," Stormfield Edition, 15:271—72.

10. *Mark Twain's Autobiography*, ed. Albert Bigelow Paine (New York and London: Harper, 1924), 1:102—3.

11. "Character Formation and Diachronic Theory," in *Social Structure: Essays Presented to A. R. Radcliffe-Brown*, ed. Meyer Fortes (New York: Russell and Russell, 1963), p. 28.

12. "The Will to Learn," in *Toward a Theory of Instruction* (Cambridge, Mass.: Harvard University Press, 1966), p. 125.

13. (Berkeley: University of California Press, 1960), pp. 134—44.

14. *"What Is Man?" and Other Philosophical Writings*, ed. Paul Baender, vol. 19, *The Works of Mark Twain* (Berkeley: University of California Press, 1973), p. 140.

15. Ibid., p. 161.

16. Ibid., p. 182.

17. *A Tramp Abroad*, Stormfield Ed., 9:107—8.

18. *What Is Man?*, p. 163.

19. Ibid., p. 459.

20. Ibid., p. 167.

21. *Partisan Review* 15 (June 1948): 664—71.

22. *Structuralism*, trans. and ed. Chaninah Maschler (New York: Basic Books, 1970), p. 5.

The Role of Drama

I

If he can, if he has anything "transcendent" in him, Twainian man in *Huckleberry Finn* responds to the pressure of situations not by yielding to the structural cycle of emotions but by turning situations into events, that is, finite temporal patterns of human action, which I will call "dramas." For some time Twain critics have been examining similar ideas. Richard Chase has spoken at length of the importance of melodrama in *Huckleberry Finn*; Roger B. Salomon, of "romance," "true adventure," and "ritual." Henry Nash Smith says, of the riverbank culture he opposes to the raft culture, "The falseness of the prevalent values finds expression in an almost universal tendency of the townspeople to make spurious claims to status through self-dramatization," that is, through self-inflation, as Smith's context shows.[1] In *Mark Twain's Burlesque Patterns* Franklin P. Rogers postulates the hoax as the basic Twain form and points out that a world of hoaxes is a man-made and bizarre world. None of these readers, however, sees dramatic behavior as part of the structural and thematic unity of *Huckleberry Finn*, or as a generative, structural principle in the novel. Chase's "melodrama" is a characteristic of tone and world-outlook; Salomon's "ritual" is to drama as bricks are to the principles of architecture and the buildings based upon them. Smith's view, like all his work on the novel, postulates a standard from which civilization has deviated, and, in this case, reduces human dramatic behavior to isolated individual acts of "fraudulent role-taking."[2]

But the whole matter is much wider and deeper than that. The critics have been chipping at the edges of something universal and overwhelming in the novel, something that not only underlies the usual social values and behavior but generates and controls them. Reading the novel, one is bothered by numerous anomalies (in addition to the ones that can be explained by the demand value of situations). At the beginning, when Huck and Tom alarm Jim outside the widow's house, why does Huck endure agonies rather than scratch his itching nose and reveal himself to Jim? Jim is not likely to make a fuss. Is it just a matter of a "game"? Or are "games" the matter of Huck's world? Why does Huck, writing the novel and looking back over his adventures, group this trivial event with funerals and other important occasions when "it won't do for you to scratch" (chap. 2)? What does Tom mean by "fun" when he says he wants to go back and "tie Jim to the tree for fun" (chap. 2)? And why does Jim later exaggerate the incident of finding his hat hung on a tree limb, and

why do the other slaves look up to him for it? Why does
Huck want to substitute Tom's brand of "style" for
the purely functional quality of the escape from Pap's
cabin? Why do the people at Pokeville camp meeting fall
for the King's absurd blarney about pirates? Why do the
mourners at the Wilks funeral "naturally" want to
know what caused the commotion in the cellar, and why
is the undertaker's *sotto voce* explanation, "*He had a rat!*,"
such "a great satisfaction to the people" (chap. 27)?
Why do the Bricksville mob forget their duty to lynch
Colonel Sherburn until they have repeatedly reenacted
the shooting of Boggs? Why does Huck put up with the
King and the Duke for so long rather than decamp
with Jim while the rascals are busy on shore? Why do
the Wilkses' neighbors prefer fake Wilks relatives to
the real thing?

   The answer in each case is the human need for drama,
the central human activity of the novel. Drama is order-
making activity, in contrast to mere activity, which is
associated with the passive response to situations.
The goal of drama is the temporary ordering of the
alternate flatness and turbulence (both unbearable) of
man's existence in nature. Permanent ordering is
impossible because life is a matter of turbulence and
change regardless of what one tries to do about it,
because men find most prolonged order boring and
therefore change it, and because in a unified world no
ordered system (e.g., the Grangerford feud) can escape
intrusion followed by instability and destruction.
The essence of drama is not the passing product but the
purposeful activity itself, the drama-making process
that leads to the temporary order. The activity, not the

completed drama, is the essence, because in and
through that activity man can resist and for a time
dominate nature; anyway, a completed drama cannot
count for anything because being completed it no longer
exists—it has become the past. The ordering can be of
separate words and things, individual situations, or
cultures (systems of values and the behavior resulting
from their applications to situations). The activity is
controlled by the law that rules *Huckleberry Finn* but that
Twain did not formulate until years later: "From his
cradle to his grave a man never does a single thing
which has any FIRST AND FOREMOST object
but one—to secure peace of mind, spiritual comfort, for
HIMSELF."[3] In *Huckleberry Finn* "peace of mind" and
"spiritual comfort" mean relief from the pressures of
"civilization" (other people's dramas) and from the
fear caused by unrelieved confrontations with nature.

Peace of mind for oneself does not imply solipsism or
completely isolated activity. Given the unity of the
world of *Huckleberry Finn*, communal interaction is in
itself a "spiritual comfort" to the characters; the dramatic
results of such interactions can be enjoyed individually.
In *What Is Man?* Twain suggests this point in a negative
way that obscures the concession to communalism:
"The [charitable] act must do *him* good, FIRST;
otherwise he will not do it. He may *think* he is doing it
solely for the other person's sake, but it is not so."[4]
What drives the drama-making character is a blind instinct
that Twain called "Will" in *What Is Man?*.[5] Thanks to
his characteristically fuzzy thinking, the power and
quality of this instinct are less stated than implied, as in
the aforementioned summary of a long reverie: "a

drifting panorama of ever-changing, ever-dissolving views manufactured by my mind without any help from me."[6]

Though the concept of drama is not presented explicitly in *Huckleberry Finn*, because of Huck's limitations as a thinker, the dramatic instinct is clearly not only what animates characters but what ranks them in their world. Drama-making activity has a double function: to organize the flux of reality, and to win status for the dramatist by demonstrating his prowess, which enables him to rise above those who can only yield to situations. This status is genuine, not "spurious" as Henry Nash Smith says: it is the basis of every other kind of status in the world of this novel. Given these postulates of drama, we can see, for example, why the mourners at the Wilks funeral must know what that racket in the cellar is, why they accept the undertaker's interruption of a solemn moment, and why they admire him less for stopping the noise than for telling them what caused it and for telling it in a certain way. As long as the reason for the noise is unknown, the dog is doing more than interrupting a tedious social ritual; he is breaking up the order provided by that ritual. The undertaker gains status not only for resolving the uncertainty but for announcing it in a stage-whisper, so that he perfects the decorum, the ordered flow, of the funeral, as he maintains the decorum. And we can see why Huck, during his escape from the cabin, emphasizes his own safety less than the way he is fooling others: creating a communal drama and putting "style" into it are more important than saving one's skin crudely. And why Tom, after dominating Huck and the whole ending,

feels free to flaunt his own rule of secrecy, and indeed
must do so, at the end of Chapter the Last. The very
superfluity of Tom's antics in the ending, like those of a
tightrope walker with his chairs and bicycles, underscores
Tom's mastery of the situation. In a turbulent world
this mastery, with its attendant gestures, must be
endlessly renewed. Because it has not been challenged
in a way that calls for a practical response, it can be
renewed only through the superfluous, "impractical"
gesture.

As one might expect from the nature of the world of
Huckleberry Finn, the need for drama is immediate and
intense to the point of desperation. Frank Kermode
understates the case when he says, "Men in the middest
make considerable imaginative investments in coherent
patterns which, by the provision of an end, make
possible a satisfying consonance with the origins and the
middle."[7] Before the arrival of the daily steamboat in
Old Times on the Mississippi, "the day was *glorious*
with expectancy"; after it left, "the day was a *dead
and empty thing*. Not only the boys but the *whole village*
felt this" (my italics). For the critic, the need for
"consonance" is a philosophical matter; for the inhabitants
of Hannibal, St. Petersburg, Pokeville, Pikeville,
and Bricksville, it is a matter of life and death. Without
drama life is only a husk, a static and empty thing. Drama
fills it, organizes it, and literally animates it. Melville's
problem of meaning, suggested in *Moby-Dick* and
explored in the shabby dramas of *The Confidence-Man*,
has been taken to its conclusion here. At Pokeville
camp meeting "the people woke up more and more"
(chap. 20), they came to life, during the singing; having

53

been dead, they were now ready to make "considerable
. . . investments" ($87.75) in the "coherent patterns"
provided by the King. The condition of despair that
prevails only at the end of *The Confidence-Man*, after the
light has been put out, has become the everyday
condition for these Twain characters. The King is
the savior of Pokeville.[8]

Behind the sameness of everyday human life lies the
sameness of nature, to which man reacts with the boredom
and fear that I have discussed earlier. The simplest
reaction to nonhuman, meaningless time and its flow
is an act of blind, nondramatic aggression: "killing."
Many of the characters kill people. Huck kills time and
thus gets a direct revenge on the medium that threatens
him. References to killing time and to the need to
kill time are frequent:

> . . . It was deadly dull, and I was fidgety. . . . All I
> wanted was a change, I warn't particular. (Chap. 1)
>
> I was 'most all the time at it [trying to escape from Pap's
> cabin], because it was about the only way to put in the time.
> (Chap. 6)
>
> . . . How slow and still the time did drag along. (Chap. 6)
>
> There ain't no better way to put in time when you are lone-
> some. (Chap. 8)
>
> I went exploring around down through the island . . .
> mainly [because] I wanted to put in the time. (Chap. 8)
>
> Next morning I said it was getting slow and dull, and I
> wanted to get a stirring up, some way. (Chap. 10)
>
> Here is the way we put in the time. (Chap. 19)
>
> "I'm jist a-freezin' for something fresh." (Chap. 20)

Most of these examples come from the early part of the novel, before Huck and his companions have more than enough excitement thrust upon them.

If boredom and lonesomeness can be eliminated—that is, if a fairly large and isolated group of people can persuade themselves that time has been killed for good —then one has a paradise on earth. The Grangerford feud and Tom Sawyer's scheme for the evasion both meet this requirement—with limitations for Huck, who is not completely inside either drama though he gets some excitement out of both, and ultimately with limitations for everyone involved, there being only so many feuders to kill and so many ways to stall the Phelpses. As narrator, Huck is able to master time by shaping it to fit a timeless entity, a book. In particular he masters time by using shaping devices like the phrase "by and by." This phrase allows him as narrator to slide over the meaningless (to him) periods of life as if they had never existed for him as character, and get to the elements that fit with each other to produce meaning for him. Huck, then, can use language as magic—which more than makes up for his embarrassing failures with prayer and lamp-rubbing in chapter 3.

The need to dominate, a primary need in the novel, is the other reason for the power of drama and for man's need of drama, and is the source of the most important type, "gratuitous" drama. By organizing his own life and the lives of others, Twainian man demonstrates his superiority to his situation in a turbulent natural world and in a human world that tries to dominate him. The need for domination is, like other forms of sadism, insatiable. No one in this novel ever has enough of dominating. Regardless of reputation or rational requirements, Tom Sawyer is driven on and on, during the ending, and the King and the Duke, at the Wilkses. "I never see such a girafft as the king was for wanting to swallow *everything*," says Huck (chap. 28), as the King tries to sell off the last unwanted bit of Wilks property (ominously, a graveyard plot). The rascals take too long; but even when the real Wilks heirs arrive and the scheme is collapsing, the King keeps right on, to Huck's amazement. The episode reveals Huck's limitations as well as the King's. Lacking the demonic force that drives men like the King, Huck cannot begin to understand him, or Buck Grangerford, or Tom Sawyer. Twain is never more like Swift, the satirist to whom he is often compared, than in this study of an irrational drive that he projects from himself. What baffles Huck about Buck and Tom is what might have baffled a more perceptive Twain about his own infatuation with the Paige typesetter: not only a willingness to throw himself whole hog into the affair but a need to spin it out and to draw more and more people into the vortex of destruction.

Huck unwittingly provides an explanation when he says that Tom walks up to the Phelps house "ca'm and important, like the ram" (chap. 33). Tom is potent; he has a natural urge to dominate and he does so—he cannot help it. Many others do the same, in their way. Jim cannot control many people, but he can shape situations on an abstract level. He at once assimilates the "dream" of the fog into his ruling mental system (his religion of superstition). When Huck tells him the truth, that it was not a dream, Jim, after great effort, assimilates the matter to his self-respect, a major part of his conception of himself.

After the hounds "bulge in" under Jim's bed, the evasion is in peril. Huck can do nothing, but Tom quick-wittedly organizes—that is, dramatizes—the situation. He gets rid of the dogs, confirms the Phelpses' slave Nat in his belief that the dogs are witches, and persuades him to see the boys' future behavior in terms of witchcraft. Greatly relieved, Huck says, "That was all fixed" (chap. 37). What follows from drama is just this feeling of relief and satisfaction, the intensity of which, like so much else in *Huckleberry Finn*, depends on the situation—the greatness of the need and the complexity of the drama. As the supreme form of human action, the only one that leads to peace and fulfillment, drama satisfies; and the bigger and better the drama, the more it satisfies, whether or not the situation is "serious" or "important" by conventional cultural standards or in the reader's expectations. Huck's escape from the cabin is a "serious" matter, and it is proper that the morning after this adventure Huck wakes up, lies quietly in the grass, and feels "rested and ruther comfortable and satisfied" (chap. 8). It is questionable, though, which is greater, his satisfaction at getting away from Pap, or his pleasure in tricking and dominating Pap and the townspeople through the "style" and "touches" of the escape. The Grangerfords, according to Buck's account (chap. 18), also felt comfortable and satisfied after killing old Baldy Shepherdson, who had killed, in the proper manner, young Bud Grangerford, who had "stopped and faced around so as to have the bullet-holes in front, you know"—a comfortable and satisfying death,

take it all around, as Huck would say. Nothing in this
episode or Buck's telling of it, however, makes sense in
terms of conventional or logical standards of behavior.
As the Duke expects, the townspeople in Bricksville go
from rage to smug satisfaction when they figure out a way
to turn their humiliation by the King and the Duke
into a deception of their neighbors. The townspeople in
the Wilks episode are, as we have seen, comfortable and
satisfied when the undertaker helps them make sense
out of the mysterious racket in the cellar.

The matter or use of the event, or the explanation of it,
must "answer." In a scene that looks utterly silly on
the surface, the boys' meeting in the cave (chap. 2),
Tom nearly loses control of his followers when he cannot
define the word "ransom." Finally he says that it means
"keep them till they're dead." Ben Rogers, Tom's most
severe critic, says, "Now, that's something *like*. That'll
answer. Why couldn't you said that before?" We can see
that Tom's explanation is absurd, but Ben Rogers
does not see it that way. For him the matter has been
cleared up and put in order. Order is what counts.
Effectiveness in ordering is everything; ineffectiveness
is catastrophe. The attack on the Sunday-school picnic
fails to "answer" for anyone in Tom's gang, and that
is why the attack is wrong. None of the boys feel any
guilt about stealing toys from small children.

Drama can be absurd or it can fail in practical terms,
yet it can still "answer," order life and divert people for
a while from the unbearable, from the mystery and
disorder of nature. This characteristic makes drama
universal in *Huckleberry Finn*, and makes the term "drama"
more useful in discussing the novel than "romance," a

term closely associated with this novel since Richard
Chase applied it in *The American Novel and Its Tradition*.
"Romance" is well defined by Roger Salomon:

> True romance was for Twain the independent struggle by a
> strong and capable individual against the forces that control
> human existence. It meant in a word, adventure—heroic not
> in its moral purity but its grandiosity, its feats of skill and
> daring, and, above all, its freedom. True romance was the
> antithesis and eternal enemy of the false as Huck was an-
> tithetical (potentially hostile) to Tom Sawyer. True romance
> was the celebration of the American folk hero; false romance
> was the perpetuation of a foreign mythology on an alien soil.[9]

This suggests drama, a man's "independent struggle
against the forces that control human existence," but limits
us to but one aspect of drama (large adventures), puts
the emphasis on the social level and the archetypal
approach rather than on internal relationships and the
psychological approach, and postulates a fundamental
hostility between Huck and Tom where I see a
fundamental similarity in kind along with considerable
differences in degree (of which more below). Slighting
the apparent trivia of the novel for the impressively
archetypal material makes it difficult to see, for example,
the deep and ominous resemblance of the boys' gang and
the Grangerford feud, of Huck's satisfaction with
his escape from Pap's cabin and his satisfaction with
the absurd complexities of the evasion.

Drama involves everyone—all ages, all classes, both
sexes, both races—and "answers" for everyone, satisfies
everyone's need to respond to the pressure of situations
and engage in reciprocally satisfying relationships. It

is this link to the qualities of the world of *Huckleberry Finn* that makes "drama" a more fully useful critical concept than Salomon's "romance," Smith's "self-dramatization," Rogers's "hoax," Boorstin's "pseudo-event," or even Twain's own term "glory" (used extensively in *Old Times on the Mississippi* and *The Adventures of Tom Sawyer*). It is in moving from one-sided hoaxes and self-centered "glory" to drama that Twain makes *Huckleberry Finn* a more profound study of man than any of his earlier novels. The world of *Tom Sawyer*, like the world of the hoax, is a Cartesian world of subject and object, of one glory-hungry youth and a large passive world for him to victimize. The world of *Huckleberry Finn* is a unit; both persecutor and victim take part in the dramas, and both benefit. Unlike *Tom Sawyer*, moreover, *Huckleberry Finn* deals not with glory and isolated adventures but with the reasons why people like Tom Sawyer seek glory and adventures.

This reciprocal, participatory quality of drama may be seen from beginning to end, even in those episodes where the dramas fail because they do not call for participation. One of the most remarkable examples of both kinds is the Pokeville episode (chap. 20). The King goes to the prayer meeting; the Duke stays in town and works in the printing office. Each man succeeds according to his real, his dramatic contribution to the satisfaction of others. Moving into a crowd that has been "woke up" and is "just crazy and wild"—that is, a group that is hungry for meaningful (dramatic) action—the King gives them a story that fits their best picture of themselves, that allows them to see themselves as "natural brothers and benefactors of the race." After the King rewards

them, they reward him. He leaves with $87.75, the kisses
of the prettiest girls, and a three-gallon jug of whiskey.
The Duke spends the day printing runaway-slave posters,
swindling farmers out of their petty cash and produce,
and setting up a romantic poem ("Yes, crush, cold world,
this breaking heart"), actions that people probably
do not want and certainly do not need. The Duke ends
the day with $9.50. The ratio of the two sums, nearly
ten to one, suggests the value of genuine drama as
opposed to simple hoax (and also to real toil, something
almost never seen in this novel).

Another ratio of values is suggested when Aunt Sally
comments on Tom's deception of her and Uncle Silas:
"I'd be willing to stand a thousand such jokes to have
you here" (chap. 33). Tom's is a straightforward
malicious hoax, but Aunt Sally does get an emotional
satisfaction out of it, plus the satisfaction of a spectator
at a play ("Well, to think of that performance!").
One might object that another victim, Boggs, hardly
benefits from being shot down by Sherburn; but Boggs
has a good deal of satisfaction at the beginning of his
episode (chap. 21), and in sum the negative (his death
and his daughter's grief) is lost in the positive (the
enormous satisfaction of the crowd and the unmeasurable
pleasure of the inscrutable Colonel Sherburn). Death,
the ultimate drama, can, as in biology, form part of a
perfect symbiosis.

Drama is not only wide but deep; it takes us to
the bedrock of culture. Culture has been defined as
"a result of individual and social striving for symbolically
meaningful experience."[10] That is, culture is drama. But in
the turbulent world of *Huckleberry Finn* drama must be

impermanent. Twain is projecting little of the anthropologist's sense of a rich culture, eternal or repeated patterns of functional rituals reflecting and satisfying the basic needs of a largely static human group. Twain gives us mostly incidents, episodes, that "answer" for the time being but otherwise have nothing in common with what went before.

In Twain's commitment to this vision of culture, he advances beyond—or perhaps retreats from—the world of *Tom Sawyer* and *The Prince and the Pauper* toward the nightmare chaos of the end of *A Connecticut Yankee* and the majority of his late manuscript fragments (the *Mysterious Stranger* manuscripts, "Which Was the Dream?," "The Great Dark," and so on). In *Tom Sawyer* the boys may raise hell with the institutions of culture and society; but these institutions are solid and permanent, and one is always aware of St. Petersburg as a going concern. The same is true of Tom Canty's Tudor England. In *Huckleberry Finn*, however, society and culture virtually disappear. We know that the South of this era was a farming region based on slavery, a powerful cultural concept. Slavery is omnipresent in this novel, but as a self-sufficient dramatic concept. Its *raison d'être*, the agricultural economy, has vanished. We learn that the Phelpses live on a "one-horse cotton plantation" (chap. 32) and that Colonel Grangerford owns "a lot of farms, and over a hundred niggers" (chap. 18), but we never see or even hear of any farming activities. The Phelpses' neighbors appear, not as working farmers, but as excited actors in a thrilling one-performance drama. Colonel Grangerford is seen in action only in his daily family ritual of greeting. The only permanent or cyclical material lies in the domain of nature, which most people avoid and which can bore even Huck after "two or three days." The only kind of natural phenomenon that can deeply satisfy Huck is a thunderstorm or a sunrise—that is, a finite event, a natural drama, with a beginning, a middle, and an end. Huck, as I have said, turns in panic from nature as flat eternity or as mere turbulence, just as the Bricksville loafers turn to sadistic sports from the endless gnawing of the river at their village. To keep himself sane, Twainian man must be less the symbol-making animal, as the anthropologists call man, than the symbolic-event-making animal. Twain's imagined world, like his real one, knew only episodes; and Huck, being Twain's creation, treats everything in his life and in his book as episodes, or tries to make situations into episodes.

Reality, then, must be organized, and the organization must reflect the nature of the world that the characters know. The boys calmly accept Tom's establishment of the gang in terms of "nothing only robbery and murder" (chap. 2), the only organized criminal activity that they know of (no doubt from legends of the Murrill gang). Huck must organize his escape as an event (a murder); the townsfolk must swallow the bait and quickly settle on a murderer; the ritual hunt for the corpse must follow, complete with cannonades and floating loaves. Only Mrs. Loftus can see the smoke on Jackson's Island—the men of her community can think only of death, not of the humdrum activities of the living. In giving Huck an identity as a runaway apprentice, Mrs. Loftus not only solves a problem but organizes the situation and assimilates it to the standard poor-white vision of life as misery. The Wilks crowd seize unerringly on a similar opportunity: it is much more fun and more meaningful to dig up a corpse by lantern light than to wait two days for the solid but dreary evidence of the Reverend Mr. Wilks's luggage. The evasion ends in an ecstasy of appreciation for a mock-apocalypse combining a slave insurrection, African witchcraft, and attacks by western desperadoes. Aunt Sally does not hesitate to explain the incompetence of the Phelps dogs in supernatural terms. The natural and true explanation—that they ran into people they knew—is literally inconceivable because it is undramatic and unsatisfying. Her judgment of the evasion—"Why, *sperits* couldn't a done better, and been no smarter" (chap. 41)—is based on the cultural sense of the power of death and the dead, and on the final importance of drama. All these incidents, and many others, reveal that importance.

The dramatic organizing must be done to satisfy the self, or a group of selves acting as one, a mob. The point is made early in the book when Huck rejects the widow's dictum that he "must help other people, . . . and never think about myself." He says bluntly, "I couldn't see no advantage about it—except for the other people" (chap. 3). This doctrine of the primacy of self-pleasing is stated quite explicitly in *What Is Man?*.[11] In *Huckleberry Finn* even the most altruistic action serves the self. It is pleasing to see Huck try to rescue the men on the *Walter Scott*, but upsetting to hear him say he is doing it "so they can be hung when their time comes" (chap. 13). In this novel even social decorum begins with self-pleasing.

That the need for drama is involved with egotism is not astonishing, but it is curious to see the need dominating real demands and benefits. Huck endures the itching of

his nose (chap. 2); he puts up with the scouring of
wooden swords because he wants "to see the camels and
elephants" (chap. 3) of the Arab caravan promised by
Tom. The judge whom Pap victimizes sets himself up
for the kill by indulging in sententious generalities; here,
clearly, is a predestined victim, a man who prefers any
organization of reality to caution and safety. Pap likewise
sets himself up for Huck's escape by suggesting to
Huck the idea of faking a murder; as Huck realizes, Pap's
obsession with killing eliminates in advance any chance
that he might analyze the escape rationally. Huck accepts
without comment the Duke's decision to tie Jim with ropes:
"Handcuffs and chains would look still better on him,
but it wouldn't go well with the story of us being so
poor. . . . Ropes are the correct things—we must preserve
the unities, as we say on the boards" (chap. 20). This
concern with immediate satisfaction and inner harmony
reflects Twain's own practice. At the height of his career,
when he was intensely money-minded and consciously
practical, he could get "6 1/2 days of booming pleasure"
from writing "Simon Wheeler, Detective," an
improvisation that he later called "witless"[12] and did not
finish or publish.

Drama even dominates being. Colonel Grangerford, we
learn, "was sunshine most always—I mean he made it
seem like good weather" (chap. 18). Huck's hasty
correction of "was" to "made it seem like" suggests that
what matters to Huck in recollection, as he writes the book,
is not the colonel's nature but his ability to project
himself into his environment and involve other people in
his mood. The colonel's methods not only are effective
at the moment but leave a powerful after-image with his
family: "When he turned into a cloud-bank it was awful

dark for a half a minute and that was enough; there
wouldn't nothing go wrong again for a week" (chap. 18).
The ease of rebirth in *Huckleberry Finn* illustrates again this
power of drama over being. To be reborn and re-created
is normal in a world where life is constant re-creation as
well as recreation. The loafers and would-be lynchers of
Bricksville fail and earn Colonel Sherburn's contempt
not just because they are what they are but because they
are only what they are and cannot change.

A less important but equally pervasive point is the
domination of drama over truth, consistency, and
probability. The reader, as much a happy victim as the
characters, accepts these manipulations because they give
him the artistic effects that he wants. Aunt Sally is at
first a spry housewife, the mother of toddlers (chap. 32);
within a few weeks she has aged twenty years and
acquired an "old gray head" (chap. 41). In the one case
she is supposed to be formidable; in the other, pitiable. No
one has objected to this contradiction in character and
appearance. No one has found it odd that two Wilks
brothers are at home in England and the other has migrated
without explanation to darkest Arkansas. The reader is in
the same situation as Joanna, the youngest Wilks sister, in
her argument with Huck (chap. 26). She does not want
truth or probability in Huck's stories about life in England;
she wants coherence, and she accepts Huck's wildest lies
when they fit a pattern. Huck himself comes down on
the side of coherence when he defends truth-telling
not because it is virtuous but because it is fairly often
more effective—"better, and actuly *safer*, than a lie" (chap.
28). That is, truth may, oddly enough, lend itself to a
beneficial order when a lie does not.

The reader benefits in the same way, because one's

world as reader is as aesthetic, as dramatic, as the
characters' worlds are. The outraged reaction of many
readers to the ending is similar in kind if not in cause to the
disgust of the characters at each others' incoherence
and dramatic failures, and to their fury at their own failures.
Huck waxes sarcastic at Pap's transparent bluster and
incompetence, while being properly frightened by Pap's
rages, the results of his failures. Huck likewise admires the
King and the Duke when they are in good dramatic form,
but despises their silly antics and bloated rhetoric at the
Wilkses: "I never see anything so disgusting. . . . It
was just sickening," and so on (chap. 25). (But we should
remember that those antics are effective with their
audience, the townspeople, just as Tom's antics
are effective with Huck and the farmers during the
ending, so that both episodes are functional and successful,
as long as they are effective.)

The need for drama varies from person to person, and
(to a lesser degree) from situation to situation. Every
one but Tom quits the robber gang when the boys fail to get
any real loot. Huck cannot afford this sort of nonsense,
because of his difficult psychological and social situation,
and the other boys do not need it, but Tom needs it and can
well afford it. Huck drops prayer when Heaven ignores
his demands for fishhooks, but Miss Watson keeps right
on with religious ritual, which helps her organize her
world so that she can righteously bully Huck and Jim.
The latter, survival-oriented by necessity, is decidedly
uninterested in departures from reality. For Jim even the
French language is a needless complication; "Why
doan' a Frenchman *talk* like a man?", he argues (chap. 14),
revealing that for him as for the other characters reality
is consistency according to the narrow world he knows.

II

The inherent power of drama, the deepest of the
structure-generating principles in *Huckleberry Finn*, explains
the characters' desire to organize existence dramatically,
and in fact explains that organizing, desire or no desire.
Twain was well aware of the workings of this power in
himself. In a striking passage in "Is Shakespeare Dead?"
he not only used ideas connected with drama as weapons
for "proving" that Shakespeare could not have written the
plays, he admitted that he had to take the dramatic
approach to the discussion of this poet. Twain recalled
that he was at first enthusiastic about Shakespeare, but:
"Then the thing happened which has happened to
more persons than to me when principle and personal
interest found themselves in opposition to each other and a
choice had to be made: I let principle go and went over
to the other side. Not the entire way, but far enough
to answer the requirements of the case."[13] "Personal
interest" is the need that drama fits. The sense of the
dramatic power, in the narrower sense of artistic power,
"the thing in me," was thrust especially hard upon Twain
after the death of Susy Clemens, when he abandoned
social life, one of his favorite dramatic media, yet was still
driven on to work.

> I like that; I enjoy it, & stick to it. I do it without purpose
> & without ambition; merely for the love of it.
> . . . Indeed I am a mud image, & it puzzles me to
> know what it is in me that writes, & that has comedy-
> fancies & finds pleasure in phrasing them. It is a law of
> our nature, of course, or it wouldn't happen; the thing in me
> forgets the presence of the mud image & goes its own
> way wholly unconscious of it & apparently of no kinship
> with it.[14]

There is then nothing belittling about Satan's final pronouncement in Paine's version of *The Mysterious Stranger*: "You are but a *thought*." This is in fact a compliment to man. Thought creates the world, Satan implies, after showing the principle in action to the boys. Nothing is more powerful than drama because reality is a series of dramas, so that there is nothing for drama to be less powerful than. Men in *Huckleberry Finn* live in a natural world that is real enough—all too real, often—but they yearn for a pure, thought-created world. Their troubles arise from the clash between the world of reality and the world of thought, and their triumphs come in those brief moments when thought manages a precarious domination over reality. Huck, in fact, insists on seeing people as characters or parts, not as actors of parts. Though Huck is sorry to see people die—Buck Grangerford, for example—it never occurs to him that he is really involved with them, that permanent effects for them might be permanent effects for him, and vice versa. It is only a step, though a long one, from the anonymous "king" and "duke" in *Huckleberry Finn*, and Huck's brief pity for their deaths, to the little people created by Satan, and the narrator's brief sorrow when Satan mashes them into the ground. And it is only a step from the gang admiring Tom Sawyer to the Eseldorf boys admiring Satan. In each case the arrogance of the drama-maker irritates the boys, but his power dominates them.

This concept of a controlling power, invisible but as pervasive as the law of gravity, accounts for much in *Huckleberry Finn*. Once released, this power takes over and operates according to its own laws, with results that also depend, like the effects of gravity, on the situation.

Drama's natural tendency is to go to extremes, to create a
world of melodrama like that of modern political extremists
and, for that matter, the American novel as interpreted by
Richard Chase in *The American Novel and Its Tradition.*
The operation of such an immaterial force in a material
world is suggested by the way Huck explains Tom's wound
to the doctor: "He had a dream . . . and it shot him"
(chap. 41). "Singular dream," says the doctor, who is
dazed by the situation, but is himself so fully controlled by
the great cultural drama, slavery, that he neglects his
regular patients rather than risk letting Jim escape.
The ending, which I shall discuss in detail later, is a process
that depends on the power of drama and generates more
power and more control as it goes. The reader, like the
doctor, must yield to the forces unleashed by Tom Sawyer
and his half-willing thralls. (A kind of hangover from this
experience perhaps accounts for some of the critical
distaste for the ending.)

The inherent power of drama has numerous side effects.
It makes people do things they otherwise would not do. In
chapter 1, where Huck is Miss Watson's victim, he
cannot sit still; in chapter 2, where he is taking part in a
drama he needs and enjoys, he can make himself lie still
and suffer agonies from his itching nose, and later can
listen reverently to Tom's nonsense in the cave. While
Huck is escaping from Pap's cabin, he wishes Tom
were there so he could "spread himself" and "throw
in the fancy touches" (chap. 7)—the situation itself does
not demand fancy touches, but once Huck has it organized
as a drama, the stylish touches are essential. The need for
the kind of dramatic experience known as "adventure"
pushes Huck aboard the *Walter Scott*, despite the fears of

Jim, who, being in a special personal situation, must
fight the force that he yielded to earlier, in the witch-riding
and hair ball episodes, for example.

The raft need go only a little out of its way to reach the
wrecked steamboat, but at other times the dramatic
power can make people go far out of their way, literally
and figuratively. Tom turns around and goes back to "fool
Jim" (chap. 2); Boggs is hurrying toward his rendezvous
with death when Sherburn steps out to shoot him. The
great power of drama makes listeners accept farfetched
explanations, the novel's most typical brief verbal dramas.
The slave-hunters are not merely ready to believe Huck's
tale of woe—they finish it for him: "Your pap's got
the small-pox, and you know it precious well" (chap. 16).
Mrs. Loftus, as we have seen, supplies Huck with the
best possible identity for his situation, and does not think
of making him prove it as she made him try to prove that
he was a girl. Jim's friends respond ardently to his
wild story of being ridden by witches, because it fits their
religious drama. At first amazed by Tom's story of the
evasion, Aunt Sally quickly assimilates it to her accepted
view, the accepted view, of boys ("harum-scarum"), so
that in the end what Huck and Tom have done is right,
not morally right, but fitting for a dramatic world. Though
Huck knows very well what the King and the Duke are,
he lets them have their way as they have their way
with each other when they reveal their noble identities.
They are all riding with the current of drama, which
reinforces the current of situation—Huck is bored, the
rascals need new identities.

In chapters 22 and 23, when Huck casually drops his
narrative of the lynching scene, turns to his long

enthusiastic discussion of the circus, derides the King's
performance of Shakespeare, and finally gives an admiring
account of the Nonesuch episode, we can see another
corollary to the law of the power of drama: effective drama
dominates truth. Huck is not bothered by the fake drunk
at the circus and fails to notice the ringmaster's faking, but
the failure of the Shakespeare show is embarrassing
because Huck is involved with the King's obvious
incompetence. By the time of the Wilks episode Huck has
become something of a connoisseur of drama, so the King's
awkwardness disgusts him; but the townsfolk, starved
for entertaining and meaningful experience—that is, for
drama—prefer the King to the real Wilks heir, not because
the King has proofs, but because the King is exciting
and the real Mr. Wilks is colorless. Despite the King's
unsuitability for his role of English minister, he pursues
it so vigorously that "he was actuly beginning to believe what
he was saying, *himself*" (chap. 29)—a sign of the difference
between drama and hoax. Dramatically effective language,
rather than honest language, dominates throughout the
ending. Huck may object to the hollowness of Tom's
language, but he goes along, always, as he must.

    When language actually bends and changes, as in the
King's bland dismissal of "obsequies" in favor of "orgies"—
"it means the thing you're after, more exact"—or the
redefining of "ransom" by Tom to mean murder,
we encounter another corollary of the power of drama:
life molds itself to fit drama. It is not simply that drama
molds life. Such an idea misleadingly implies passivity.
Following the law of reciprocity, men work with each other
toward mutually desirable goals. If changes are needed to
create or impose drama, and if changes can be made, then

they will be made. A presumptuous or aggressive dramatist will lean on life unnecessarily at times, just to remind others that he can. The King changes "obsequies" to "orgies"; Tom changes "picks" to "case-knives." In each case others go along. Generally the changes to reality are made or helped along spontaneously and eagerly by participants in dramas (not by victims of hoaxes, as adherents of the hoax-theory would say). When changes are not made eagerly, they are at least made. Harvey Wilks starts off confidently enough ("I am Peter Wilks's brother Harvey, and this is his brother William"); but the crowd prefers the King, and the King has hypnotized himself and them into believing that *he* is Harvey Wilks, so that a few pages later the real Harvey is constrained to say, "Is there anybody here that helped to lay out my br— helped to lay out the late Peter Wilks for burying?" (chap. 29). Poor Harvey cannot call his brother his brother any more; he must yield to the demands of the dramatic situation. There is hardly a more striking example of the power of drama to soften and remold.

Yielding to drama can be unwilling. Jim bows to the boys again and again; in fact, he bows to every one (white) in the novel, not because he enjoys the situations he is put into (he commonly feels "powerful sick" during them), but because he, being black and a slave, is always cast in a subordinate part. His real needs as a person do not matter, do not exist, because as a person he does not exist. People (whites) who do want and need drama can do amazing things to make others yield to it. Before Boggs is shot (chap. 21), he disappears, only to reappear suddenly, "a-reeling across the street towards me bareheaded, with a friend on both sides of him aholt of his

arms and hurrying him along." Boggs is being hurried
toward Colonel Sherburn, not away from him. We know this
because Huck, after observing Boggs, has to turn around
("I looked over there") in order to see Sherburn. Sherburn
aims at Boggs, the men jump to one side, and Sherburn
fires, violating his own vow to shoot Boggs only if Boggs
bothered him again. Who are these "friends"? Why
are they "hurrying him along"? Boggs, as Huck notes, is
"doing some of the hurrying himself," no doubt under
the drunken impression that he is being taken away from
Sherburn. These "friends" are deliberately hurrying
Boggs along to the final act of his tragicomedy. If they did
not take charge of him, he might wander off and escape
what they have come to regard, with his help, as his destiny.
The desperately bored and drama-hungry townspeople
must have the shooting of Boggs; they cannot risk its not
happening.

The depth of their hunger is well suggested by the scene
that follows the death of Boggs. Every dramatic
possibility of the killing is used and reused and savored and
exhausted of meaning. Only after that does the crowd
remember its manners and become a lynching mob. The
immediate power of drama is suggested in this seizing
first on the immediate and available materials for
drama-making rather than the biggest and most
"important" but distant ones. The attempt to lynch
Colonel Sherburn is itself wholly dramatic, as Sherburn's
speech suggests. There is contempt in the speech, but no
anger; he knows that the crowd is just excited and
not hostile—in the latter case they would subordinate the
public and dramatic aspects of the affair and come masked
in the dark. The crowd is, really, grateful to the colonel

for reminding them ("The idea of *you* lynching anbody!") that they are playing parts for which they are ill-suited. They are out to kill time, not the colonel.

Human groups in this novel are all "mobs"; they are all formed and controlled by the power of drama. "The town," as Huck calls it, has a similar temporary corporate quality in the Wilks episode, as does the Phelpses' neighborhood in the ending. The people at Bricksville, being on permanent holiday, have an excuse for being available for mob duty. The other groups have no such excuse; like the Grangerfords, they seem to have economic functions, but in reality exist only to supply actors and choruses. In the Wilks episode there are a few, like the lawyer Levi Bell and the "husky" Hines, who stay in the world of reality, but the town rejects them as it rejects the real Wilks brothers. The farmers in the ending are all pulled into the current of the evasion, and are kept there first by their close physical grouping in Aunt Sally's parlor and later by the exhortations of the chorus of farmwives. Huck has been pulled in from the beginning of the evasion, because the power of the gratuitous drama necessarily directs him away from his colorlessly practical plan to walk into Jim's cabin and walk out with him.

Drama even controls perception, the most elementary human contact with natural reality. Mrs. Loftus sees the smoke on Jackson's Island because she has no need, as others do, *not* to see it, and because she is a newcomer to the St. Petersburg area. The old inhabitants do not see the smoke. We get a glimpse of the reason when Mrs. Loftus says that someone told her "hardly anybody ever goes to that island over yonder that they call Jackson's Island" (chap. 11). The local people, imprisoned in their narrow communal "knowledge" that nobody lives on the island, cannot see what their eyes are looking at: smoke from a fire made by someone living on the island. The ignorant newcomer can see it.

Like folkways and folk-knowledge, dreams and stories are part of the large world of drama, and blind people the same way. Even after Huck points to the trash on the raft as concrete proof of the falsehood of his story, Jim is still dominated by it: "He had got the dream fixed so strong in his head that he couldn't seem to shake it loose and get the facts back into its place again, right away" (chap. 15). Likewise Huck cannot shake loose the impression that Colonel Grangerford makes on him. The long description of the colonel (chap. 16) is loosely organized and never used directly. The colonel is simply *there*. Rather than blame Twain for this, as Richard Bridgman does,[15] it would be better to blame Huck. The colonel's appearance is his drama, his "thing." Huck is as hypnotized by the colonel's act as Jim is by Huck's "dream" and the St. Petersburg people by what they think they know about Jackson's Island. The length of Huck's description suggests his fascination. He begins in a neutral way ("Col. Grangerford was very tall and very slim") and describes the colonel's manner rather anxiously at first ("when . . . the lightning begun to flicker out from under his eyebrows, you wanted to climb a tree") but ends on a cheerful and affectionate note. This process recapitulates Huck's actual experience, from neutral observing, through the conflicts of acculturation, to full acceptance of the colonel's standards and manner. Having once accepted Colonel Grangerford, Huck must describe him at length later (when he is writing at the

Phelpses); many other aspects of the Grangerford culture
(such as the way they ran their farms) are not described,
because Huck has not really seen them, has not absorbed
them dramatically.

Huck perceives the King and the Duke more simply and
naïvely, making his troubles with them all the more
disturbing, to him and to us. When Huck first sees them,
they are fleeing from a mob. Assuming that all outcasts are
like Jim and himself, Huck helps the two strangers
without question. After the Wilks episode, when the
rascals fail at every trick and begin to "talk low and
confidential" in the wigwam, Huck and Jim do not "like
the look of it," but are far from anxious for themselves.
"We made up our minds they was going to break into
somebody's house or store, or was going into the
counterfeit-money business, or something" (chap. 31).
Huck has shared so much with these men and gotten
so much excitement out of them that, despite his knowledge
of them and his fresh memories of the Wilks episode
and its aftermath, he cannot believe that they will use
him as raw material.

Huck's blindness to the intentions of the King and the
Duke is paralleled by his frequent blindness to nature.
The critical interpretations of the force of nature as
myth in *Huckleberry Finn* ignore the wide fluctuations in
intensity of the treatment of nature as environment.
This level of intensity is not an independent variable; it is
rather a function of the real independent variable,
drama. Nature is a secondary reservoir of drama; it
commands attention when nothing of interest is going on in
the human world, and is ignored when something is going on
there, because that something is drama. During two

leisured intervals Huck describes thunderstorms in great
detail and with obvious relish (chaps. 9, 20). A thunderstorm
is, as I have said, an event, highly "dramatic" in more
ways than one. While the mob is digging up Peter Wilks's
coffin (chap. 29), another thunderstorm gathers that
Huck notes periodically and that forms a functional
background to the action (the lightning shows Huck an
unmoored boat for his escape). But "them people never
took no notice of [the storm], they was so full of this
business." Perception of nature, that is, is in inverse
relation to absorption in drama—a good example of the
self-regulating nature of structures. On the raft Huck
is doing nothing and can fully appreciate storms; in the
graveyard Huck is still doing nothing but has a vital
interest in what is happening and places the storm in the
middle background; the mob around the Wilks grave is
totally occupied and sees no storm at all.

It is much the same with the level of specificity of
descriptions arising from Huck's other contacts with nature.
When Huck and Jim are under pressure, they notice only
what they need to notice in nature; but on the flooded
Jackson's Island they notice every small detail because
they have nothing else to do (chap. 9). Huck indulges in
the long, marvelous description of the sunrise because
for "two or three days" he and Jim are completely at
ease, following their narrow escape from the Grangerfords
(chap. 19). Only occasionally does physical nature (the
river) enter directly as a dramatic force (e.g., the fog
episode, Huck's two encounters with panic), and it is in
such scenes that we have "the great brown god" of
T. S. Eliot and other critics. When Huck is absorbed in
human events and affairs—the camp meeting, Tom's gang,

the murder of Boggs, and the foolery of the evasion—he
shows no awareness of nature or weather. We can feel
the warmth and humidity of the raft voyage because
Huck tells us that he and Jim "was always naked, day
and night, whenever the mosquitoes would let us" (chap.
19); but the state of the weather during the last quarter
of the novel can only be inferred from Huck's remark,
"We was down south in the warm weather, now" (chap.
31), and from a few other clues like Huck's complaint
about the heat of the roomful of farmers (chap. 40).
Settings also interest Huck only as part of dramatic events.
Pap's cabin and the Phelps farm are described in detail
because the dramatic events that happen there require a
close knowledge of the terrain. The Grangerford parlor
is not the setting of any action, but is described minutely
as part of an elaborate dramatic construction, the
Grangerford "style."

III

The power of drama, which dovetails with the need for
drama, generates the dramas themselves. These are
of two types, survival drama and gratuitous drama. The
two resemble each other in structure, since every drama
must have certain characteristics to be effective, but differ
radically in the most important aspect, function. Survival
dramas are devised for physical survival. Huck's escape
from Pap's cabin is the classic example. Successful
survival dramas give little satisfaction. Huck feels less
pride in escaping from the cabin than in escaping in
"style." Gratuitous drama is the reorganizing of a situation
to give it meaning and divert everyone present from
the horrors of nature and time, which otherwise could

drive the characters involved into boredom at best and
panic at worst. Gratuitous drama is thus a kind of survival
drama too, keeping one's sanity being a form of survival.
Because gratuitous drama has no immediately obvious
necessity, it is open to attack by readers (and by
characters, like Huck at the Wilkses) for being mere
hoax or time-wasting. Gratuitous drama is also a kind of
celebration of the dramatist's physical and social
security, as Huck implies in his awed comments about
Tom's taking the lead in stealing Jim (chap. 34).

Gratuitous drama takes two forms, artificial and
functional, or ineffective and effective. All drama is
literally "artificial" in the sense that it is made, but
artificial drama in this novel is artificial in the
pejorative sense—contrived, awkward, and unrewarding for
its audience or its victims. Henry Nash Smith mistakenly,
I think, attacked all drama-making in *Huckleberry Finn*
as the making of "spurious claims to status through
self-dramatization,"[16] an apt description if limited to the
artificial gratuitous drama. Typical of the really artificial
kind are the ones Huck is unprofitably involved with
in the opening chapters: Miss Watson's sadistic
Puritanism (a private drama); the "robber gang" in its
later, unsuccessful stages; the operations, like prayer
and lamp-rubbing, that involve useless efforts to carry out
other people's unexplained instructions. These things
do kill some time—the central job of any drama—but
they are true hoaxes, they often involve bullying, they
bore quickly, and they leave a sour aftertaste that in
Huck's case makes him grateful for the change forced on
him by Pap.

The functional gratuitous drama does not bore, when it

is at its peak. Such a drama, no matter how silly or
crude to the reader, works for the characters involved—
the dramatist on one side, the audience or participants
(more properly the latter) on the other. Such a drama
arises from the characters' situations in time, space, and
social rank, enlists all their talents and energies, and
satisfies, for a time, the deep need for order that I have
discussed above. The flow of meaning from traditional
culture has dried up; what is left behind is a litter of
empty shells to be used as the containers or stages of
gratuitous dramas. The basic structure of social status—
the division into the quality, other whites, and black slaves
—still survives, but only in relation to drama; the quality,
headed by Tom Sawyer, Colonel Sherburn, and the
Grangerfords, define themselves by their dramatic skill
and impudence, and the other classes take their places
below. The traditional American harmony of home, school,
and church exists to be derided as "civilization," and,
in the case of the church, abandoned to the hogs (chap.
18). The Phelps culture exists so that "Sid Sawyer"
may take it apart and rebuild it as a set for his greatest
drama, the evasion. This evasion and the earlier feud
are parodies of culture, monstrous self-destroying
machines. The Wilks funeral is not a decorous ceremony
in and through which the townsfolk come to terms with
death; it is a drama, a diversion from the boredom of
village existence. The dominant emotions are the people's
macabre curiosity about that racket in the cellar, and
Huck's and the reader's excited awareness of that bag
of gold on the breast of the corpse. The body of Mr. Wilks
is not treated with the dignity and ceremony traditionally
given the dead; it becomes a toy in an exciting game,

"Who's the Real Wilks?" The Dionysian uproar of
camp meetings served real purposes in the semi-frontier
of Twain's youth, but in *Huckleberry Finn* it serves only
to stimulate the people of Pokeville to bamboozle
themselves.

One powerful continuous drama of culture, slavery,
has, however, survived to serve Twain's purpose. Slavery
is so pervasive that paradoxically it disappears, like the
oxygen in the air, while continuing to affect everything.
For the reader slavery is therefore an impressive cultural
force, and cultural structure, but only up to a point.
Since slavery was a completely historical phenomenon,
dead twenty years before publication of the novel, one
can hardly react to it as a timeless concept. There were
still rafts and Wilks funerals in the 1880s, and these
things are still imaginable today, but slavery died in
the 1860s and cannot return or be reimagined.

This central kind of drama, the functional gratuitous
drama, is of three basic sorts: dramas of action, appearance,
and language. I will discuss these three sorts at some
length, classifying the most complex sort, the dramas of
language, in terms of intricacy. I will then try to show
that dramas can be approached profitably in terms of
intensity, the amount of conscious pretense involved,
audacity, and finally the basic criterion of effectiveness.

The most common sort of drama in *Huckleberry Finn*
is the drama of action, in which one or more characters
try to create meaningful events or try to shape events to
make them meaningful. The great example is the evasion,
in which Tom Sawyer tries to reshape an entire world.
When I use the term "drama," especially in talking about
structure, I usually mean the drama of action. Of the three

sorts of drama the simplest is the drama of appearance,
of which Colonel Grangerford provides the best example.
In himself he is a work of art, and without uttering a
word he can produce great effects. That is why Huck
describes him at such great length and hardly mentions
him otherwise. In contrast, all we know of Colonel
Sherburn's appearance is that he is "a proud-looking
man about fifty-five—and . . . a heap the best-dressed
man in that town" (chap. 21). Sherburn is a different
kind of dramatist from his fellow colonel, and we are given
just enough about Sherburn to sense his position in
relation to Boggs and the lynching mob but not enough
to remove the air of inscrutability that surrounds him
and makes him frightening. The primacy of action for
Sherburn is demonstrated in the baldest way when he
shoots Boggs without justification or Sawyeresque "style,"
turns on his heel, and walks off—a gesture of contempt
for everything that is not pure action.

In the lynching scene, though, Sherburn shows us the
breadth of his talents by doing little and saying much,
with this result: " 'Now *leave.*' . . . The crowd washed
back sudden, and then broke all apart and went tearing
off, every which way" (chap. 22). Here is a major kind
of gratuitous drama, the drama of language, of which
there are several types. I will look at them in terms of
their levels of complexity. Twain himself was a master
of the dramatics of appearance and an eternally hopeful
experimenter in that form of dramatic action known as
"business"; but the center of his life was dominating
others through rhetoric, and he projects that emphasis
into *Huckleberry Finn.* The most potent talkers among the
characters are the most potent dramatists, and vice versa,

though it is well to remember that the most successful
dramatist, Colonel Sherburn, is also a silent man of
action—Twain's ultimate hero, a combination of himself
and General Grant. Almost every character in the novel
can use language with some skill; Twain could not
project himself into inarticulate McTeagues. Buck
Grangerford, a mere boy, defends the feud brilliantly;
the youngest Wilks girl, the "harelip," cross-examines
Huck with tenacity and skill. The greatest talkers are
the most memorable characters: Pap, the Duke, the King
(at times), Colonel Sherburn, Tom, and Huck himself,
the writer of the book.

"One cannot insist too much on the verbal quality of
Huckleberry Finn," says Richard Bridgman, quite rightly.
He has examined in detail Twain's subtle and extensive
use of linguistic oddities and distortions, his "placement
of familiar words in unfamiliar situations, . . . his
repetitions of sounds," his repetitions and associations
of words in order to create resonances and cross-references.
Bridgman approaches the verbal level of the novel
principally from the point of view of the author at work,
though of the King's first speech at the Wilks house,
Bridgman says, using the limited approach of hoax-
critics, "The king's words are florid, full of spurious
rhetoric. . . . As such they successfully represent the
fraudulent confidence-man at work."[17]

I approach the language of the novel in terms of its
relation to the dramatic dynamics of the novel. The
"stylistic activities" of the King and others are forms of
drama. Their function is less to communicate than to
organize and to dominate. They dominate by projecting
a verbal organization onto the flux of life, and they

maintain that organization and domination through
the devices that Bridgman mentions. There is nothing
"spurious" or "fraudulent" about all this, or, to put it
another way, human activity as Twain projects it here is
all "spurious" and "fraudulent." The power here of the
American vernacular reflects the importance of language,
and the place of language, in American culture. American
vernacular forms, says a pioneer student of American
civilization, "represent the unself-conscious efforts of
common people to create satisfying patterns out of the
elements of their environment. . . . It is the art of
sovereign, even if uncultivated people. . . ."[18] When
everyone is a sovereign, then those "satisfying patterns"
are bound to be sovereign themselves.

On the simplest level language dominates through the
energy behind it. On this level sense is secondary (or,
even more secondary than it is elsewhere). Language
usage here is a violation of the law of entropy, first a
focusing of energy, and then a maintaining of that focus.
Talking is, as I said of drama in general, a kind of
tightrope-walking that dominates onlookers as illogically
and completely as the circus dominates Huck. A successful
speech or sequence of speeches in *Huckleberry Finn* may
be nothing but energy.

The great example here is the raving of Sister
Hotchkiss, one of those Twain characters we glimpse
only for an instant but who are unforgettable just because
of their raw power. A sample, which begins with her
interruption of a man who seems ready to go on for some
time himself:

"You may *well* say it, Brer Hightower! It's jist as I was a-
sayin' to Brer Phelps, his own self. S'e, what do *you* think of it,

> Sister Hotchkiss, s'e? think o' what, Brer Phelps, s'I? think o'
> that bed-leg sawed off that a way, s'e? *think* of it, s'I? I lay it
> never sawed *itself* off, s'I—somebody *sawed* it, s'I; that's my
> opinion, take it or leave it, it mayn't be no 'count, s'I, but sich
> as 't is, it's my opinion, s'I, 'n' if anybody k'n start a better one,
> s'I, let him *do* it, s'I, that's all. I says to Sister Dunlap, s'I —."
> (Chap. 41)

This speech contains only one item of conventionally useful
information, the reference to the sawed-off bed-leg, and
this is really the contribution of Mr. Phelps, not Sister
Hotchkiss. Anyway, her point is so elementary—that
the leg did not saw itself off—that the speech is a parody of
communication. In a positive sense the speech is a
demonstration of power gained through energy. Sister
Hotchkiss organizes skillfully and, when necessary, with
subtlety. She lessens the effect of her interruption
of Brer Hightower by making it a compliment and by
referring gracefully to the host, Brer Phelps. Once she
has taken command, Sister Hotchkiss drops her pretenses
and launches into a line of nonsense-patter designed to
keep the floor and the attention of the crowd for herself
alone. The last half of the speech, one long garbled
breathless "sentence," is nothing but defiance of the
audience, and an assertion of the primacy of energy over
logic, as if to say, "If you dare and if you can, knock me off
my tightrope." Colonel Sherburn's speech is a suave
version of the same thing (see below, pp. 138-39).

   This use of energy is the foundation of all the great
speeches and the dominating element in dialogues and
general conversation, even if they make conventional sense
too. Miss Watson's speeches ("Don't put your feet up
there, Huckleberry") are notably "sensible" and flat—one
reason why she fails with Huck. Tom's manner of

speaking, well illustrated the night of Miss Watson's failure, is energetic at all times—one reason why he dominates Huck and the novel. It is significant that when the boys get to the cave, Tom speaks first and unequivocally: "Now, we'll start this band of robbers and call it Tom Sawyer's Gang" (chap. 2). "Everybody was willing," says Huck; no one dares to meet Tom's challenge.[19] Once his domination is established, Tom never relaxes his grip. When the boys offer logical objections, like Ben Rogers's complaint about keeping watch over prisoners who are going to be killed anyway, Tom crushes them with short, decisive sentences ("Kill the women? No—nobody ever saw anything in the books like that"), cadences that suggest the spurious authority of modern advertising ("Yes! Four out of five doctors agree . . . !").

At a higher level of the drama of language are the imitations that gain their power through alignment with established authorities and roles carefully chosen for the occasion. These include many of the memorable passages in the novel, especially the speeches of the King and the Shakespearean rantings of the Duke. That butchered version of Hamlet's soliloquy in chapter 21 is so tiresome to modern readers that they may not try to understand Huck's open-mouthed admiration of it. But that speech does fit. We should recall first the dominance of situation in the novel (Huck has nothing to do but watch this novelty). We should note that the speech is not merely an *absurd version* of Shakespeare, but an absurd version of *Shakespeare*, the poet whom the world admires most, so that the passage becomes a Twainian debunking of the bard, as well as satire of the period's love of bombast.

The King's flamboyant speeches are easier to take
than the Duke's. It is easier to admire the King's repentant-
pirate style (chap. 20) and his mournful-uncle style (chaps.
24 ff.) because we do not bring complex preconceptions
to these modes as we do to Shakespearean acting.

A higher rhetorical form still is the argument, the
drama of dialectic. It is easy to ridicule many of the
wrangles—Tom and the boys in the cave, Huck and Jim
arguing over the French language, Tom and Huck
disputing the aims and details of the evasion. But these
arguments begin to make sense if we see them not in terms
of their rubbishy content but as exercises in drama or as
series of ritual dramas of conquest. The cave episode is
not about robbers but about who is boss. What eventually
discredits Tom is the failure of the attack on the Sunday
school, not the immorality of the attack or the arrogance of
his manner throughout the episode. The disputes on
the raft and during the evasion are really about power.
Huck indirectly suggests this point when he rationalizes his
failure with Jim in the discussion of French: "I see it
warn't no use wasting words—you can't learn a nigger to
argue" (chap. 14); that is, the occasion is, or should be, not
one of legitimate dialectic ("words") but one of carrying
to its end a racist drama in which Huck wins because he is
white and therefore strong and intelligent and Jim
loses because he is black and therefore weak and stupid.
At this point Huck accepts unconsciously the power-
relationships of the slavery system (and since he is writing
after the events of the story, we can assume that he
still accepts them). Jim's powerful speech about the trash
on the raft (chap. 15) and Huck's silent acceptance
of it mark a turning point in their relationship: the white

listens to a brilliant speech by a black, accepts it, and later passes on both the speech and his humiliation to the world at large. The arguments between Huck and Tom during the evasion are similarly a matter of power. In these exchanges much of the outcome depends on differences in style that reflect dramatic talents and attitudes. Huck speaks soberly and directly; Tom uses the devices of rhetoric—repetition, variation, balance, antithesis—and charges his phrases with his ruthless energy.

> "Here's the ticket [says Huck]. This hole's big enough for Jim to get through, if we wrench off the board."
> [Tom says:] "It's as simple as tit-tat-toe, three in a row, and as easy as playing hooky. I should *hope* we can find a way that's a little more complicated than that, Huck Finn." (Chap. 34)

And:

> "Don't you reckon I know what I'm about? Don't I generly know what I'm about?"
> "Yes."
> "Didn't I *say* I was going to help steal the nigger?"
> "Yes."
> "Well then." (Chap. 34)

These exchanges, fairly early in the evasion, lead to ones in which Huck says less, and Tom says more and says it even more vehemently. When Huck objects, Tom pounces on him instantly; and even when Huck is fertile with his objections, as in the argument over Jim's tin plate (chap. 35), Tom is more fertile with overwhelming answers. This pattern repeats one established during the argument with Buck Grangerford about the feud (chap. 18). As in the conclusion of Strauss's *Till Eulenspiegel*, force pounds

at weakness until weakness is reduced to monosyllabic
answers and finally to silence.

The book itself is the ultimate demonstration of language
as energy focused gratuitously for power. The book is
Huck's drama, his gesture of power, and his writing style is
his "style," in the Tom Sawyer sense, the stamp that
Tom puts upon his actions as a defiance of time and
death. Nature may be potent and terrifying; with its ally
time it may "gnaw" away everything, eventually; but
it cannot talk, and Huck can. The novel is his violation of
entropy. As the omnipresent, the first and the last,
talker in the novel, Huck is as far above momentary talkers
like the King as the King at Pokeville is above a mere
toiler like the Duke. Huck himself can abandon his own
style for the style of others, as in the sanctimonies of his
reverie in chapter 31; but he always returns to his own style,
the ground base of the novel. As gratuitous drama, the
book is supreme. Even Colonel Sherburn has more reason
to kill Boggs than Huck has to write this book. At the
beginning we may feel that Huck is writing to correct
Twain's "stretchers" in Tom Sawyer. Huck's book quickly
develops its own momentum, however, and like the
evasion becomes a serious presentation of world-outlook
and values.

Huck's canny observations of others are less a matter of
sympathy than of evocation and artistic practice. By
noting that, for example, lights in cabins late at night mean
sickness, Huck indicates and sharpens his powers of
observation. At the end Huck refers directly to writing:

> Tom's most well, now, and got his bullet around his neck on
> a watch-guard for a watch, and is always seeing what time it
> is, and so there ain't nothing more to write about, and I am

rotten glad of it, because if I'd a knowed what a trouble it was
to make a book I wouldn't a tackled it, and ain't agoing to no
more.

The last part of this suggests the seriousness and effort in
the novel; the first part suggests what Huck is up to
with all that effort. Tom is doing thus and so, "so there
ain't nothing more to write about." Huck's logic is strange
unless we take the novel as a presentation of man and
his situation in a certain kind of world; then we may realize
that once the presentation is made, there is no reason to
repeat it. Having already seen in detail Tom's conceit and
dramatic power, we need see no more of it; and having
also been shown that Tom is the most conceited and potent
character in the novel (Huck, as writer, is not wholly
in the novel), we cannot benefit from seeing anyone else.
That Huck can so easily drop the potent Tom demonstrates
Huck's ultimate power and the ultimate gratuitousness
of his drama, the book. People can be brought to life and
discarded at his whim. When he is not thinking
about them, they do not exist, as Jim does not exist during
several episodes. When Huck changes his way of talking
about people, they change in essence, as Jim changes
from human being to toy during the ending; there Huck
says much about Jim's hours as a toy and little about
Jim's still numerous hours as a human companion—and
nothing at all about Jim's solitary hours as a frightened,
imprisoned slave. We are only a short distance from
Twain's ultimate dramatist, Satan, who creates people and
then literally rubs them out, and finally tells the boys
that everything they know is their own mental creation.
  These are the three significant types of dramas.

Classifying dramas in terms of major characteristics and
ranking them within those characteristics reveal
important qualities of the novel. If one ranks dramas in
terms of intensity, at the bottom come the small gestures
that amount to no more than affronts to nature, the
equivalent of Twain's pet loathing, the scratching of one's
initials in famous public places (see *The Innocents Abroad*).
Much of this dramatic activity is petty, spiteful
destructiveness, true "time-killing." It is associated with
the less important and (or perhaps because) less competent
characters: the Bricksville loafers bully sows; Pap rips
up Huck's little picture that he got "for learning my lessons
good" (chap. 5). Trivial though such gestures are, they
can have great effect in the right situation. The King's
mulish insistence on staying at the Wilkses and selling
off that last little graveyard plot leads to his downfall.
Huck's handling of the snakeskin—a presumably
trivial gesture of indifference toward witchcraft—leads him
and Jim into disaster upon disaster. A concentration of
small gestures at one time can add up to a formidable
whole. For example, Bricksville. The disgusting people,
the mud streets, the shabby houses, the filthy yards, all are
affronts to the higher levels of drama, in particular the
basic idea of social decorum. Nature will, of course,
win in the long run, after it has "gnawed" at the town long
enough; but in the meantime, in the middest, Bricksville
is always with us. Bricksville the physical environment is
produced by Bricksville the anti-society, and helps
produce it. This anti-society is a system of affronts.
The loafers jeer at each other and destroy life; Boggs jeers
at Huck, the stranger, and Colonel Sherburn, the leading
citizen (both of whom should be treated with special

courtesy); the colonel contemptuously destroys Boggs and sneers the lynching mob into submission; Huck, under the spell, treats it all with casual indifference. The Duke, after failing with Shakespeare, catches on. He bases the primary appeal of the Nonesuch on the crude salaciousness of the townsfolk, and the continued working of the hoax on their eagerness to "sell" their fellow citizens the same way they have been "sold."

The highest level of continuously available dramatic framework is the religion of witchcraft that governs the novel. It is supreme, and more powerful than Christianity, because it gives meaning and order to all of human experience, including cruelty. Christianity, as these people know it, has to do more with the dead than the living, and as Huck says, "I don't take no stock in dead people" (chap. 1). In a world of passing situations and limited dramas, the historical sense disappears and only pigs feel comfortable in church. Christianity cannot explain the snakeskin for Huck, or the spirit voices and the hounds for Nat, the Phelpses' slave. Witchcraft is even better—broader, more orderly, more dependable— than Tom's system of authorities. Witchcraft, then, is what students of society call a superior "conceptual map." Beside this advantage its disadvantage—the fear it creates and strengthens—is trivial.

Dramas can also be ranked according to the amount of conscious pretense involved. At the bottom is "letting- on," open pretense; it is useful as an emergency measure to save a larger drama. "Letting-on" occurs during the evasion, the largest drama in the book, when it becomes clear to Tom that the whole affair is about to collapse. If the boys continue digging with case knives, they will not reach him quickly enough to maintain unity of time; if they simply walk in Jim's front door, as Huck suggests, they will have abandoned the whole drama. Tom solves the problem with a compromise. He demands a pick, saying, "There's excuse for picks and letting-on in a case like this; if it warn't so, I wouldn't approve of it, nor I wouldn't stand by and see the rules broke." With picks the boys are able to dig Jim out in a couple of hours. We sniff at this and sympathize with Huck when he says, "Picks is the thing, moral or no moral"; but within the world of the novel it is Tom who is right, or at least decorous, and Huck who is indecorous and therefore second-rate. Huck himself agrees implicitly with this evaluation; he does not object to the letting-on and admires Tom for being "full of principle" (chap. 36).

At the other end of the spectrum of pretense come the dramas that are utterly sincere and also successful. Tom's efforts with the robber gang are sincere enough but poorly related to reality. The feud is much better, and the evasion is best of all because it fits into an aspect of the greatest cultural drama, slavery. So great is the southern fear of a slave revolt that even the most preposterous details of the evasion are not questioned once that fear is tapped. In this state of autointoxication even a generally rational character like Aunt Sally can instantly warp natural phenomena to fit the fantasy structure. When, surrounded by hysterical farmers, she notices a yellow liquid trickling down from under Huck's hat, her mind ignores mundane explanations and selects the idea of brain fever from the most melodramatic level of illness she knows.

Drama can also be evaluated on a scale that measures

audacity and extremism. The more extreme a drama,
the more effective, provided that the execution is minimally
acceptable (and if the preposterousness becomes a little
too obvious, there is always "letting-on" as a cure).
After Huck tells an improbable story justifying his relation
to the situation on the *Walter Scott*, his audience, the
watchman on a ferryboat, exclaims, "My George! It's
the beatenest thing I ever struck" (chap. 13). This is the
reaction that Huck needs. If the story were less "beaten"
and the watchman not beaten down by it, he might ask
embarrassing questions rather than help Huck. The
Shakespearean show put on by "Mr. Garrick" and "Mr.
Kean" fails ludicrously because the two rascals cannot
carry it off. The circus, in contrast, carries off its faking
with professional smartness, and Huck, along with the
crowd, accepts all of it without question. The hoax of
the Nonesuch, likewise, is based on assumptions so
daring and execution so perfect that it cannot help
succeeding. A full-length obscene show would leave its
audience satisfied but, once the euphoria had worn off,
ready to lynch the King and the Duke for putting on
an obscene show. The Nonesuch, as presented, is long
enough to interest the crowd, but short enough to make
them feel cheated and react to the cheating rather than
to the obscenity. The Wilks episode does fail, but not for a
lack of audacity, which the King displays with success
in the very teeth of the facts. The later failures of the
rascals, at dancing schools and "yellocution," result from
their failure to reach minimum standards of competence:
"they didn't know no more how to dance than a kangaroo
does" (chap. 31).

The final criterion, as I have said, is effectiveness,

"answering." The opening of the novel, usually slighted, is of crucial importance, because it is there that Huck learns this basic principle of dramatic effectiveness. In a few pages he becomes involved in personal and cultural dramas, limited and continuous dramas, high-pressure and low-pressure dramas. In experiencing them, he develops patterns of response that he follows throughout his later experiences. He rejects Miss Watson's "pecking" not only because it is unpleasant but because it does nothing for him; on the other hand he accepts the Widow's tactful "civilizing" pressure because it satisfies basic physical needs (like warmth in winter) and opens up areas of personal advantage, like the ability to read, without asking too much of him. Huck rejects prayer because he can "see no advantage about it" (chap. 3)—that is, it is ineffective as drama—and because Miss Watson will not solve this problem of effectiveness for him. According to Richard Poirier, Huck condemns Tom's "games" in the opening chapters,[20] but it is clear that Huck condemns not the games but their occasional ineffectiveness. Huck enjoys the early phases of the robber gang. He appreciates the logic, the dramatic logic, of the criminal ideas Tom spouts in the cave, and fails to note the absurdity of their content. Huck is "most ready to cry" (chap. 2) when he cannot produce a parent to kill so that he can join the gang. Killing a parent is an effective dramatic touch in a boys' group founded in a cultural situation of parental meddling and severity like Twain's St. Petersburg, which in these opening chapters is still the St. Petersburg of *The Adventures of Tom Sawyer*. The idea of patricide "answers." Questions of ethics and possibility are irrelevant. Huck quits the

gang only when he can "see no profit in it" (chap. 3). He
criticizes Tom's story of the genie and the lamp on
the ground that there is nothing in it for the genie (he
instinctively takes the side of the enthralled), but he
does decide to give lamp-rubbing a chance to show its
effectiveness for him. "I . . . rubbed and rubbed till I
sweat like an Injun, . . . but it warn't no use. . . . I
judged that all that stuff was only just one of Tom Sawyer's
lies. . . . It had all the marks of a Sunday school"
(chap. 3). At the end of the novel, when Tom invents an
effective drama that has none of the marks of a Sunday
school, Huck goes along with it despite his numerous
reservations. Likewise, when the King and the Duke are
smooth and successful, Huck puts up with their faults;
when they are ineffectual and nasty, he turns against
them at once. Effectiveness is always the ruling principle.

Thinking in terms of the laws of drama and dramas,
a critic can begin to make sense out of the farcical elements
of *Huckleberry Finn*. Many readers have felt uneasy
about the snake episode in the ending and indeed about the
entire ending; such elements have often left an unpleasant
aftertaste, a feeling that Twain is not really a serious
writer. But farce is pattern, and pattern is what is wanted in
the world of drama. The old hierarchy of modes is
replaced in this novel by a hierarchy of dramatic
effectiveness. Some of the farcical scenes, like the antics
with snakes and rats in the ending, can be attacked on
the ground that they are poorly done and therefore
ineffective as the author's (Twain's) work; but within the
novel, as the characters' actions and Huck's work, such
scenes may be effective and significant.

Farce, as an easily practiced mode, is a handy shelter for

Twainian dramatists. As Eric Bentley has noted in his stimulating discussion of farce in *The Life of the Drama*, style is essential to successful farce.[21] And certainly style is central to the world of *Huckleberry Finn*. Yapping dogs and shouting women greet Huck's uncertain approach to the Phelps house; a few hours later, silent and respectful attention greets Tom's "ca'm and important" approach to the same house. Bentley points out further that a major element of farce is hostility, handled of course with style, else the art of farce is a mere exhibition of sadism.[22] Given the world of *Huckleberry Finn*, where domination is everyone's goal and everyone's fear, where the only coherent cultural behavior is enslaving and killing, nothing else but farce can be suitable as a basic art form. To feel as Henry Nash Smith does, that the ending of this novel should properly be tragic,[23] is to require that Twain violate his own artistic decorum.

IV

The Twainian "dramatist" is not an actor; drama-making must be distinguished from role-playing. The characters usually act out their own dramas, and often create them as they go along, but the creation of the dramatic concept and the ordering of reality around it count more than the acting. Tom Sawyer creates the drama of the robber gang attacking the rich Arabs, but the part he plays in the debacle of the actual attack is not mentioned. At any rate the plan collapses because it is no good, not because Tom's acting is no good. Both the King and the Duke act at Pokeville, the Duke all day, the King for a few minutes. The rewards go to the King, who gives satisfaction to the most people, not to the Duke, who tries the hardest. The rascals' later successes, especially the Nonesuch, are the responsibility of the Duke, generally the more able dramatist of the pair; their failures come from their error in allowing the King to take over the planning in addition to acting the major roles.

But in *Huckleberry Finn* Twain, then at his own worldly peak, usually shows us good dramatists and their characteristics. The master dramatist first of all embodies the greatest quality of Twain's ironic ideal, Satan:[24] he *knows* man and the world, man's permanent nature and the world's mutability. With Colonel Sherburn he can say, "I know you through and through," and he has Sherburn's ability to grasp situations and to make up actions to suit. This is gratuitous drama, the highest type. Dramatists can be graded according to their dramatic practice, along a scale from survival drama, the basic but unprestigious form, to the gratuitous type, which, as I have said, is a gesture demonstrating the dramatist's superiority to questions of survival. At the top of the scale is Colonel Sherburn, the dramatist's dramatist, nonchalantly killing Boggs in the key example of pure gratuitous drama, and then turning a survival situation, the lynching scene, into a harangue that demonstrates again his domination of his world. Tom Sawyer is very high on the scale and gets so much exposure that he is over-all the major dramatist of *Huckleberry Finn*. Poor Boggs, squashed for daring to try a little gratuitous dramatizing, is at the bottom, only a little below the mass of Bricksvilleans. Huck, who fails except as a survivalist, would be near the bottom too, were he not able to produce the ultimate gratuitous gesture, a book.

One's degree of security parallels and determines his

place on the dramatic scale. Those whom the situational world of the novel has made secure can afford the dramatic gestures that demonstrate their security. The relationship of security to drama arises from Twain's own yearning for security and assurance great enough to allow him to do anything and evade any responsibility—a godlike state he projected into his Satans and other "strangers," and embodied in the conscience-killing psychopathic narrator of "The Recent Carnival of Crime in Connecticut," written only a few months before *Huckleberry Finn* was begun. In the highest dramatic gesture of personal security Colonel Sherburn, after killing Boggs, drops his gun and turns his back, thus abandoning two basic safeguards in his dangerous world. (One recalls that one Grangerford, Bud, was shot down when unarmed, and another, Buck, was shot from behind.) Pap, the opposite pole from the colonel, pays with his life for his strutting and swagger. Slaves, by cultural definition, are totally insecure as persons and secure only as property; they stick to survival drama, and they survive. Compared with Jim or any slave, Huck is relatively secure. Add to that the truth that he really is more secure with Jim on Jackson's Island than with Pap in the cabin, and he develops the self-delusion that launches him into the episodes of the snakeskin, Mrs. Loftus, and the *Walter Scott*—disasters all. At the very end of his adventures, when Huck really is secure for the first time in his life, he is finally able to indulge himself at length, and he does: he writes a book.[25]

As the most secure and the most potent character, and an often-seen one, Tom is the major dramatist of the novel. (Colonel Sherburn is more potent, but he appears for

only a few pages.) An early version of the Prometheus-
Satan-Prospero figure, Tom brings the sacred fire, the
fascination and magic of drama, to Huck, the other boys in
the gang, Aunt Sally, and Sister Hotchkiss and her
friends. Tom is marked for what he is in his first
appearance (chap. 2): he *goes back* to trick Jim and to
steal candles. Many characters in this novel would try to
avoid the situation, as Huck does; others might play
tricks if the situation offered itself; Tom creates his own
situations. He turns back, makes up the trick on Jim, and
plays it. In aggressiveness the King and the Duke
resemble Tom, but they are his inferiors at spotting,
establishing, and maintaining long-term dramas (and they
lack his secure social status). Tom is also superior in his
ability to extend the weaponry of drama to include books
that matter to his victims. His "authorities" are authorities
not just because they are books but because they truly
have authority over people, even if the authority is spurious.
Some books fail, even the greatest, as the King and the
Duke learn when Shakespeare, badly acted, is a flop at
Bricksville. In contrast Tom's unnamed "pirate books and
robber books" (chap. 2) serve, when used with Tom's
manic energy, to dominate the other children in the gang
and to regain control after Ben Rogers trips up Tom
on the meaning of "ransom." The use of "authorities" is
not in itself a perfect weapon. Tom is shown this primary
lesson, though he is blind to it, in the latter part of the
evasion. There he works less from his own ideas, which
were quite effective in the early part of the episode,
and more from the "authorities." They conflict with the
situation, already exacerbated by the panic he himself has
created, and the result is a narrow escape from catastrophe.

Tom's wildness in the evasion is a sudden release of impulses thwarted previously by lack of opportunity. Jim, in contrast, can never know any such frustrations or any such release. Within his situation as a slave, the drama forced upon him, his religion is big enough to be all-absorbing most of the time, and satisfying enough to keep him content. Tom's paying Jim "forty dollars for being prisoner for us so patient, and doing it up so good" (Chap. the Last) shows Tom's realization that "being prisoner" is an acting job for Jim and no more than that. From a humanistic standpoint the payment of Jim is shameful, because no one can repay him for the humiliations and absurdities that have been forced upon him. From a dramatic standpoint, though, the payment suggests Jim's practicality, which is so foreign to the novel and hence absurd.] During the ending Jim, as a passive helpless victim, *is* absurd, as victims are in farce. Even when Jim is a free agent, he is a highly unsatisfactory collaborator in drama—not good at "argument," overcautious or else not cautious enough (it is his suggestion that Huck dress up like a girl and visit Mrs. Loftus).

But when he is working in his own areas of competence, Jim is a success. Saying he knows "most everything" (chap. 8), he lavishly explains natural signs, which are everything he knows and therefore "everything." Huck loses interest in the Loftus episode once it is over, but Jim offers a shrewd analysis of the probable actions of Mrs. Loftus and the posse she sends out. Posses are something slaves must care about. Earlier, in the hair-ball episode, Jim dazzles Huck with his expertise and his concluding harangue that covers all possibilities for Huck's

future without committing Jim to anything. But at the
end Jim goes outside his realm of mastery and escapes
disaster only through luck: he plays the part of an
honorable man and gives himself up to save Tom's life.
Having violated the rule of situation, which does not allow
Jim to join in the dramas of white men, Jim is doomed to
reenslavement until he is released by the *deus ex machina*
of Miss Watson's deathbed act.

Like Huck the character, Huck the artist is a mixture. As
the maker of the novel, he dominates it totally; but in
the action he makes, he is for the most part either a
spectator or a victim, and when he joins in gratuitous
dramas, he usually reveals his incompetence. He thus
reflects Twain's duality about himself in relation to the
world and his habit of treating that duality ambivalently.[26]
Huck is an artist, but he is ineffectual in worldly
affairs; Huck is ineffectual in worldly affairs, but he is an
artist.

Within his limits Huck is a sharp and analytic observer.
He cherishes and uses his perceptions, such as they are.
He follows James's advice to be one on whom nothing
is lost—to which we should add the comment, based on a
more modern psychology, that a great deal is lost before
Huck begins to perceive. Students of Huck's
perceptiveness have not only overrated it but have tended
to deal with it as a limitless quantity of virtuous behavior
rather than as an artistic trait operating strongly within
narrow limits. Huck's eye for the artificiality of the
Grangerfords' fruit is noted,[27] but not Huck's failure
to disapprove. There is nothing virtuous about Huck's
description of the chalk fruit, or of the crockery animals
that squawk but do not "look different nor interested"

(chap. 17). Huck is as cool and detached as the animals. He is observing for the sake of observing.

This stance of the cool artist is his dramatic form, his "style," at once his attitude and the stamp his attitude puts on material. He notes that the lights in cabins at night are beside sickbeds; he describes a sunrise with care and precision. Just as Tom shows his immersion in the drama of action by turning back to play tricks on Jim, Huck shows his own kind of immersion by stopping the action to describe minutely this trick and Jim's own drama based upon it. Later, as I have noted, Huck controls his first encounter with Pap by observing him calmly (chap. 5). These are gratuitous observations that correspond to the gratuitous dramatic actions of others, and they succeed for the same reasons, because they are "needless" and therefore demonstrate Huck's superiority to mere contingency, and because they are handled (written) skillfully.

Huck's facile role-playing is the sign in him of the human plasticity that is one of the essentials of drama. He senses this plasticity and its cause when he says to himself, "There ain't no telling but I might come to be a murderer myself, yet, and then how would *I* like it?" (chap. 13). This is not to say that Huck is in practice a perfect artist. He has a tendency toward exaggeration. In mulling over his discovery that at times truth is better than a lie, he says, "I never see nothing like it" (chap. 28), a slovenly vernacular hyperbole that does his point no good. And Huck loses his artistic coolness in moments of anxiety and frightening novelty—leaving Jackson's Island, boarding the *Walter Scott*, watching the annihilation of the Grangerfords.

104

Huck's artistic stance must be considered apart from his
inferior behavior and achievements. The gap between
stance and behavior follows inevitably from the lack of
analytic power, of intelligence in the Jamesian sense,
that keeps him from being truly the redeemer of the
human race. Curiously, he is intensely aware of dramas and
dramatists of action and language, and of his own
inadequacies as dramatist, yet he cannot make use of his
knowledge to improve his performance. All this is
consistent with Twain's deterministic theories and his
sense of his own inconsistencies and inadequacies, but it
ruins Huck. After realizing the dishonesty of the King
and the Duke, Huck justifies his passivity toward them by
thinking, "If I never learnt nothing else out of pap,
I learnt that the best way to get along with his kind
of people is to let them have their own way" (chap. 19).
Huck fails to foresee the consequences of this decision, or
later to connect the consequences to the decision, or to
see the glaring fact that his own escape from Pap
contradicts this policy of passivity. Nor does Huck realize
that he stays with the rascals less because he is afraid
of them than because he admires them, and it is only when
he no longer admires them that he stops trying to get
along with them. When Tom turns up at the Phelpses,
Huck compares him to a ram and with no more than a
token struggle yields him the control of Jim's escape. Far
from being weak here, Huck is perceptive and decorous:
Tom is a "ram" and Huck is not. But Huck never thinks
about the consequences, for himself and Jim, of this
acceptance of reality, and the result is near-disaster for all.
In Twain's world to live decorously in accord with the
nature of man is to court failure, given the nature of man.

But the *Walter Scott* episode teaches Huck quite clearly
that he had better not try to succeed in the world—the
world, that is, of gratuitous drama. Huck does nothing
"wrong" in this episode; he does nothing, in fact, except be
there, and the supernatural intervention (removing the raft)
is thus all the more clearly a lesson. Huck is already
aware, though, of his lack of dramatic potency. When he
fishes out the baker's bread that the searchers float on the
water (chap. 8), he concludes that the prayers of "the
widow or the parson or somebody" sent it there, so that
prayer works for them; "but it don't work for me, and I
reckon it don't work for only just the right kind." The
"right kind" are those with potency, those who can pray or
rub a lamp or walk up to a house, and get what they want.
Huck's failure is reinforced in the short time between
his arrival at the Phelpses and Tom's arrival. Huck's
rebirth as Tom is a favor that the situation grants him—for
half an hour. "Providence" has told him that to rescue
Jim he must have Tom's wits and brutality. The real
Tom Sawyer then arrives "like the ram." The favor of
"Providence" has been withdrawn; role-playing must yield
to the real thing. Again we should realize that Huck's
submission to Tom here is not the weak submission of a
noble natural man to a sadistic lunatic, but rather
the respectful bow of mediocrity to talent and energy.
Within himself Huck is not natural after his decision to "go
to Hell" (chap. 31), that is, to become a criminal in his own
terms. In his relations to others he cannot be natural
either, at this point, because to everyone except Tom and
Jim, he *is* Tom Sawyer.

As a practicing dramatist Huck has several major faults.
Again, he is not analytic enough, as the Loftus episode

teaches. Before he goes into Mrs. Loftus's cabin, he says, "I made up my mind I wouldn't forget I was a girl" (chap. 10). Voluntarism, however, is an inadequate substitute for training and talent, a point that Huck would have ignored but for Jim's nagging. Huck forgets what he is doing and badly fails Mrs. Loftus's simple tests. Afterward he refuses to analyze his failure, but continues to work on the basis of impulse and instinct ("Providence"). As I said earlier, passive drifting does not help one to succeed in the situational world of this novel; and it is the worst possible way to practice drama, which calls for relentless energy and alertness. Having yielded to Providence the moment before he enters the Phelpses' yard, Huck is in trouble the first time he must think up information to give Aunt Sally rather than choose between answers she suggests. She asks him where his steamboat went aground, and his instinct says "she would be coming up—from down towards Orleans" (chap. 32). Fortunately his quick thinking enables him to evade the question entirely. Active intelligence shows itself superior to instinct: an axiom that helps to explain Tom's domination of the conclusion. The real "Providence" or ruling force of life is not at all what or where Huck thinks it is, but is rather the nature of the universe revealed in the nature and relationships of situations and of men, and Huck cannot read the signs.

In part Huck's passivity and incompetence follow, as is proper in this novel, from his situation. As a lowly figure in his world, and acutely conscious of his "mudcat" status, Huck has not been able to practice dramatics and develop confidence and skill, as Tom has. Huck's desire has been crushed; he just wants to survive, and the occasional flickerings of his dramatic instinct only serve, as we have seen, to show the wisdom of his usual practice. Twain's thinking here is unconsciously Marxian. He emphatically associates dramatic potency with the ruling social group. Through his Sherburns and Tom Sawyers, as well as in books like *The Prince and the Pauper* and *A Connecticut Yankee*, Twain shows us that "ruling" is drama and drama is ruling. And in showing us that Huck is not merely passive but incompetent, Twain suggests the scheme, explicated in *What Is Man?*, that man's fate is determined not merely by "training" but by "temperament." The rulers gain skill by ruling, but become rulers through talent. Unfortunately, Huck's undeniable literary talents are irrelevant to ruling.

1. Chase, *The American Novel and Its Tradition* (New York: Doubleday, 1957), pp. 1–41; Salomon, *Twain and the Image of History* (New Haven, Conn.: Yale University Press, 1957), p. 87; Smith, *Mark Twain: The Development of a Writer*, p. 117.

2. *Mark Twain: The Development of a Writer*, p. 118.

3. *What Is Man?*, p. 136.

4. Ibid., p. 133.

5. Ibid., pp. 199, 201.

6. Ibid., p. 182.

7. *The Sense of an Ending*, p. 17.

8. Revealing the limits of a critical method based on folklore and local color, De Voto concludes that the King's pretending to be a pirate tarnishes "the reality of a fine scene" (*Mark Twain at Work*, p. 91).

9. *Twain and the Image of History*, p. 87.

10. Gertrude Jaeger and Philip Selznick, "A Normative Theory of Culture," in Robert Meredith, ed., *American Studies: Essays on Theory and Method* (Columbus, Ohio: Charles E. Merrill, 1967), p. 117.

11. Pp. 133, 136, et passim.

12. Samuel L. Clemens to W. D. Howells, 4 July 1877 and 21 January 1879, in *Mark Twain–Howells Letters*, 1:188, 246.

13. Stormfield Ed., 26:302.

14. Samuel L. Clemens to W. D. Howells, 23 February 1897, in *Mark Twain–Howells Letters*, 2:664.

15. *The Colloquial Style in America* (New York: Oxford University Press, 1966), p. 126.

16. *Mark Twain: The Development of a Writer*, p. 117.

17. *The Colloquial Tradition in America*, pp. 112 ff.

18. John A. Kouwenhoven, *Made in America: The Arts in Modern Civilization* (Garden City, N. Y.: Doubleday, 1948), p. 14.

19. Opening sentences are often crucial; consider Colonel Sherburn's cowing of the mob with his first sentence, "The idea of *you* lynching anybody!" (chap. 22), or the doctor's soothing of an angry crowd, "Don't be no rougher on him than you're obleeged to, because he ain't a bad nigger" (chap. 42).

20. *A World Elsewhere: The Place of Style in American Literature* (New York: Oxford University Press, 1966), pp. 181 ff.

21. *The Life of the Drama* (New York: Oxford University Press, 1964), p. 251.

22. Ibid., pp. 219 ff.

23. *Mark Twain: The Development of a Writer*, pp. 114, 132 ff.

24. See Gibson, *Mark Twain's "Mysterious Stranger" Manuscripts*, pp. 14–19; Coleman O. Parsons, "The Devil and Samuel Clemens," *Virginia Quarterly Review* 23 (Autumn 1947): 595–600; Coleman O. Parsons, "The Background of *The Mysterious Stranger*," *American Literature* 32 (March 1960): 55–74.

25. Eric Solomon has dealt with the novel as a search for security, rather than a gesture of security; see "*Huckleberry Finn* Once More," *College English* 22 (December 1960): 172–78.

26. The classic example is Twain's conception of his speech at the Whittier Birthday Dinner (17 December 1877) and his oscillation afterward between feelings of triumph and self-disgust; see Henry N. Smith, " 'That Hideous Mistake of Poor Clemens's,' " *Harvard Library Bulletin* 9 (Spring 1955): 145–80.

27. Tony Tanner, *The Realm of Wonder*, p. 157.

A Structure of Dramas

I

In one sense *Huckleberry Finn* is situations and dramas, but
in another sense it is some kind of a whole. Clearly it
is not a well-articulated structure in the Aristotelian sense—
only a few of the dramas, like Pokeville, and the
Nonesuch, are that—but even if it lacks such a structure, it
does begin, it does have a middle section, and it does
stop. That sounds like a parody of traditional literary form,
and indeed it is one of Twain's aims to deny the reader
the comforts of conventional form, to make him experience
chaos along with the characters, and thus to make him
accept drama as the characters do. I will discuss below the
reader's experience of the book. Before looking at
Huckleberry Finn from outside as the reader sees it, it is
necessary to look at what on the inside makes it a whole—
that is, to look at Huck as the narrator.

In this novel about a turbulent situational world it is
Huck whose presentation and embodiment of it provide the

only continuity. The formal qualities of Huck the
presenter dominate and determine the archetypal qualities
of Huck the embodiment of traits, as the opening and
closing paragraphs of the novel suggest. At the beginning
Huck shows himself aware of a subtle but major
problem of presentation, that of the dependence of
truth-telling on precision: " 'The Adventures of Tom
Sawyer' was made by Mr. Mark Twain, and he told the
truth, mainly. There was things which he stretched, but
mainly he told the truth. . . . It is mostly a true book, with
some stretchers, as I said before" (chap. 1). Huck is
a conscious, concerned narrator, and he knows that he
is doing something special and final. At the end, after
what we can take to be a sustained effort to tell the
truth and avoid "stretchers," Huck is relieved: "So there
ain't nothing more to write about, and I am rotten
glad of it, because if I'd a knowed what a trouble it was
to make a book I wouldn't a tackled it and ain't agoing to
no more" (Chap. the Last). And Huck never did;
Twain never did use him again in a major, serious work
of fiction.[1]

When Howells observed that *Huckleberry Finn* was a
"romance" because Huck was made able to tell his
story,[2] he sensed that Twain was not writing local color
or escapism but creating an unusual artistic strategy
and a problem that draws attention to the strategy. The
first-person narrator is inherently a distancing device.[3]
Huck can offer us none of the "guidance" for which
Wayne Booth prays in difficult fictional situations.[4]
It is not that Huck is distant or fails to discuss problems.
He often confides in "you," with whom he assumes
he has a good deal in common, but he fails to clarify basic

problems and pursue implications. Why is he so concerned about "stretchers"? Why, after learning through experience the difficulties of writing a book, does he continue to the end?

In working toward answers to these questions, it is necessary to keep in mind that Huck *is* the maker of the book. It is easy to forget or to ignore this point, thanks to Twain's guile. The novel is written at the Phelps house while Tom is recovering from his wound during a period of a few weeks after the evasion. There is only the one brief reference to the writing of the book itself ("there ain't nothing more to write about"), and that reference is followed and dominated by Huck's grumblings about the general difficulties of writing books. One is led to remember the difficulty of writing and forget the fact of writing. The short interval between Huck's experiences and his writing makes impossible the reflective passages and even the general air of contemplation that stamp a book long-considered (by the narrator) and then "done," like those other first-person American classics, *Moby-Dick* and *The Great Gatsby*. The opening of *Huckleberry Finn* is not suggestive of Huck's role as maker either. "Me" appears in the opening line, but with reference to Huck the character in *The Adventures of Tom Sawyer*, not Huck the writer living after the events of *Huckleberry Finn*. The writer discussed in the opening paragraph is Twain, not Huck. The word "Huck" does not appear until the sixth paragraph, where Huck is brought in not as a writer or narrator but as a passive character squirming in the clutches of Miss Watson. The full name "Huck Finn" does not appear until chapter 2.

The novel begins with such subtlety that it is almost impossible, especially in normal non-critical reading, to realize the shift from reflection and summary to the actual narrative itself. After commenting on *The Adventures of Tom Sawyer* in the first paragraph, Huck summarizes its ending in the second paragraph, and then, in the third, begins to summarize the post-*Tom Sawyer* events—that is, the events of *Huckleberry Finn*—in such a way that no one who had not read *Tom Sawyer* could tell which events are which. The paragraph shift is a signal, and to be sure Huck opens the book with a warning —"You don't know about me without you have read a book by the name of 'The Adventures of Tom Sawyer' " —but Huck follows that with the disarming comment, "but that ain't no matter." The summary-exposition of the third paragraph ("the old thing commenced again") leads to the details of what was wrong with the widow's typical meal, and a general comment, in the present tense, on the right kind of meal. We are apparently still in the area of the general, but now a new paragraph begins: "After supper she got out her book and learned me about Moses and the Bulrushers. . . ." Without warning and thus without thought we have moved from the static general past to the dynamic immediate present, the present of fiction, in which the book remains until the last paragraph of Chapter the Last. Twain thus interlocks (1) general past, (2) general timeless present, and (3) specific fictional present. His method can be contrasted with the decided manner in which initial reflections are separated from the body of the work in *Moby-Dick* and *The Great Gatsby*. Twain minimizes Huck's role as judging outsider; Melville and Fitzgerald emphasize the double positions of Ishmael and Carraway.

We get few other clear glimpses of Huck as external
maker of the book. After Buck Grangerford is killed,
Huck moves to the writer's present to comment on
the traumatic effects of the incident on him. Otherwise
Huck's position as maker is visible only indirectly
through his comments, which put us only a little out
of the flow of the novel and then only for a moment. For
example:

> The sky looks ever so deep when you lay down on your back
> in the moonshine; I never knowed it before. (Chap. 7)

> We said there warn't no home like a raft, after all. Other
> places do seem so cramped up and smothery, but a raft don't.
> You feel mighty free and easy and comfortable on a raft.
> (Chap. 18)

The second quotation rises to a high level of generality,
but, like a similar passage in chapter 19, it ends a
chapter, so that its summary, "so much for that" quality
is appropriate to the context, and the remark does not
draw attention to its violation of narrative decorum. A
similar generalization—"It was a dreadful thing to see.
Human beings *can* be awful cruel to one another"—does
not end a chapter, so that the remark stands out sharply.
  As the maker of the whole book, Huck is also the maker
of its language, the third great unifier of the novel after
the narrator and the elements of deep structure. This
language, as I have said, is a made thing, a unified
artistic creation—not "vernacular" but the illusion of
vernacular. The natural vernacular, actual speech, *arguementative*
is incoherent, repetitious, and boring.[5] At no point is
Huck's narrative style incoherent, repetitious, or boring.
Even at its more freely associative, in the reverie in

chapter 31, for example, it is coherent. In many of the most admired passages of *Huckleberry Finn* the narrative style is highly but unobtrusively organized. Consider the often-quoted sunrise scene (chap. 19). Aside from representing the idyll element stressed by T. S. Eliot and other critics, the scene is the representation of a natural drama, the sequence of sunrise ending in the temporary stasis of "the full day." The sequence, simply by being a sequence, looks like vernacular, because the vernacular, the "and then" style, is primarily sequential. But the subsections of Huck's description are subtly ordered; for example, "by-and-by you could see a streak on the water which you know by the look of the streak that there's a snag there in a swift current which breaks on it and makes that streak look that way." Here *which* and *that* are used deftly and unidiomatically to make the sentence communicate a complex idea. Our attention is skillfully diverted from the grammatical complexity by the unusually "bad" grammar as well as by the conventional use of short words. We are accustomed to think, as the Concord Public Library thought, that "bad" grammar is the major sign of vernacular speech, whereas we are beginning to understand that really "common" speech is characterized first of all by slovenliness and dishonesty. Huck, as a writer, can be accused of neither of these faults; Twain of course cannot be either.

But even if one accepts that Huck unites the novel by being its sole and complete maker and by creating its language, it is still not clear why he does it. Why does he put up with that "trouble . . . to make a book" and a literary language? Or why, barely literate and utterly ignorant of book-making, does he start to write a book in the first place? To answer "literary convention" is merely to look at the question from another point of view. I see two reasons for Huck to write his novel: to purge himself, and to create his own supreme drama.

After Huck describes the murder and mutilating of Buck Grangerford, he adds, "I wished I hadn't ever come ashore that night, to see such things. I ain't ever going to get shut of them—lots of times I dream about them" (chap. 18). The novel can be seen in one light as Huck's attempt to purge himself, to "get shut of" not only what happened to Buck but of what happened to Jim, Pap, the King, and the Duke—in short, to everyone— and beyond that, to "get shut of" what man is like, including Huck himself, for what he has to worry about most is what he did to his friend Jim.

Huck is right in saying, "There ain't nothing more to write about." Once he has gotten down what he did, while keeping his role as speaker as unobtrusive as possible, there is truly nothing more to write about. Huck makes his attempt as best he can, but purgation is impossible, as Huck recognizes in the comment on Buck's death. First Huck *wishes* he "hadn't ever come ashore that night, to see such things"; then in the present tense he answers himself in the negative: "I ain't *ever* going to get shut of them" (my italics). The situation is a paradigm. Coming ashore is moving through the world, either, the sentence ambiguously suggests, to encounter human suffering involuntarily, or in order to search for it sadistically. "That night" is all of time, including the ending, after which "there ain't nothing more to write about"—that is, the burden of life cannot increase but does not decrease. "Such things" is the suffering he

encounters, or the suffering he seeks in order to inflict
it on others. The situation and Huck's despairing
acceptance of his misery and guilt suggest Twain's own
dark mood and foreshadow his darkest late manuscripts,
which alternate between the feeling that men suffer
unjustly and the feeling that they create sufferings for
which no amount of guilt can pay. The people on those
endless dream voyages, though, never need to "come
ashore" because "such things" come to them, in the form of
storms and sea monsters, which are, from the other
point of view, a kind of sadistic and masochistic wish
fulfillment.[6]

The writing is not, however, a total failure as a gesture
of defense. Before Huck shifts to the present of writing
and starts using "now" ("Tom's most well now"),
the last thing we learn in novel-time is that his father is
dead. This puts an end to the list of Huck's fears
(Miss Watson, the King, and the Duke have preceded
Pap). But Huck has already learned how to cope with Pap
through art. When he first sees Pap at the widow's,
Huck realizes he is no longer "scared of him worth
bothering about," though Huck "used to be scared of him
all the time, he tanned me so much" (chap. 5). Huck
does not understand or say why Pap no longer frightens
him; certainly, the threat of tanning is still there (and
amply fulfilled later). But Huck says, "I stood a-looking
at him" and presents what he sees. In and by this long
description Huck triumphs finally over Pap. Huck's
defense is his ability to master the threat of the memory
of Pap with words, words like "There warn't no color
in his face, where his face showed; it was white; not
like another man's white, but a white to make a body

sick, a white to make a body's flesh crawl—a tree-toad white,
a fish-belly white." The whiteness, so Melvillean in
its impact, can "make a body sick," but Huck is not
just "a body," anybody—he is an artist. With each of the
unnecessary virtuoso phrases he displays and celebrates
the artist's defense against fear—here the greatest
fear, the fear of the death that Pap carries in his face.

In a sense, then, the novel is Huck's attempt at
purgation; but because, as Huck implies, purgation is
impossible, and because Huck lives in a world where
action is life and stasis is death, we can see the novel as an
action, Huck's action, his defensive gesture. The novel
is, in other words, Huck's drama, which not only tells
us about his impossible situation and his guilt but tells us in
an organized way—that is, artistically—so that the
impossible is put at arm's length and becomes bearable.
That Huck's drama takes the form of a verbal construction,
a lyric cry, follows from the nature of his burden. The
Bricksville loafers, those model characters, have their
boredom and deal with it physically; Huck has his
memories and can only deal with them verbally. Here he
is his father's son: Pap's burden, as his harangue about
the "govment" shows (chap. 6), is his memory of
insults to his peculiar self-respect and of his failures to
deal adequately with them, and the harangue itself is
his verbal drama of defense against those memories.

As a dramatic gesture the novel can be placed, as
I have said, in the few weeks following the evasion, when
the hullabaloo is over and Huck for the first time since
that gloomy evening at the widow's (chap. 1) has a chance
to sit down and think things through. The novel thus
dramatizes a special mood. What Huck gives us is not a

photographic and phonographic record, but *his* record, of
his experiences from the end of *Tom Sawyer* to the
present time following the evasion. On another level,
that of Twain's presentation, the novel may seem to be a
record, but on Huck's level the materials of the novel
must be considered as matters of artistic choice.
Such comments as "You feel mighty free and easy and
comfortable on a raft" must be seen as written after
the action and as representing a backward displacement
of Huck's feeling at the end. Every other element in
the book is similarly but less obviously chosen to be a note
in Huck's lyric cry.

This is not to say that the choice is conscious. Huck
is, after all, the projection of a writer who was
knowledgeable about the smaller techniques of storytelling
but notoriously inarticulate about the deeper meanings of
his most serious work. The Twainian obsessions, like
"conscience," are no more than the tip of the iceberg;
the description of Huck as a boy with "a sound heart and a
deformed conscience" is a faint clue rather than a
final explanation.

In chapter 1 Huck projects his desperate need to speak
unverbally, to dramatize the undramatizable:

> . . . The wind was trying to whisper something to me and I
> couldn't make out what it was, and so it made the cold shivers
> run over me. Then away out in the woods I heard that kind
> of a sound that a ghost makes when it wants to tell about
> something that's on its mind and can't make itself under-
> stood, and so can't rest easy in its grave, and has to go about
> that way every night grieving.

Like the wind and especially like the ghost, Huck, in his
weariness and anguish, must try to tell us something but cannot

in so many words. The wind and the ghost do communicate their feelings well, however, and likewise the novel, as a dramatic gesture, "tells" us what Huck cannot tell us explicitly. "The cold shivers" is an adequate response to the novel, but a response few readers want or can bear.

From the inside the book is Huck's; from the outside it is Twain's and the reader's—a set of strategies, for Twain, that cause a series of experiences, for the reader. Twain's over-all strategy is to leave the reader, or to force the reader to find himself left, in possession of that "nameless something," that dumb truth, communicated directly through the experience of the book, which Twain told Howells was the essence of any really good work of fiction. In the tradition of the poker-faced, malicious western humor that Twain had made the origin and foundation of his art, the novel introduces itself briefly and enigmatically—in the two prefatory notes—and then proceeds with apparent aimlessness to force the reader to make a fool of himself and thus not just to see but to experience and to internalize the "nameless something"—Twain's sense of the world and of man trying to live in, and deal with, that world. The reader sees a turbulent world of situations that provoke reactions (flight, participation) designed to satisfy emotional needs but themselves creating further emotional needs leading to further activities, and so on and on in an endless chain. The reader sees the irresistible need to make the activities in the situations sequential, and he sees the power that these temporal organizations ("dramas") have once they are begun. Twain shows us all this, and depends on the reader to make it satire by reference to moral norms. Tom's obsession with climbing that lightning rod demonstrates not only the power of drama

and the need for drama but the absurdity of dramatic man,
whether he is Tom breaking his neck or Huck resolving
the impasse by suggesting that Tom climb the stairs and
"let on" that they are the lightning rod. Huck's comment,
"Human beings *can* be awful cruel to one another,"
as he watches a redneck drama of revenge, the tarring
and feathering of the King and the Duke, places
Twainian man squarely against the central norm of
Western, Christian culture, but it is up to the reader to
make the satiric connection. Huck sees no connection; he
thinks that he has made an original discovery. Beyond this
showing and stimulating of judging, neither of which
is enough to make this novel great, lies the level of the
book as a unity, a single experience for the reader.

The highest meaning of the novel lies in the reader's
outraged response to it, the central part of that response
being the usual resentment of the ending. Without
committing himself or forcing us, Twain allows us to
identify contentedly with Huck; then he disillusions us,
and we howl. This alienating effect—or more properly,
process—is a meaning of the novel. For this process
all of the book is essential, but, to repeat, the meaning
does not exist in idylls or social satires or other static
elements. In the process Twain parodies the traditional
quest, so that satire and action are one. A traditional
quest begins with certainty and passes through uncertainty
and suffering to a new, earned certainty; *Huckleberry
Finn*, on the other hand, begins with a demonstration of
uncertainty and a process of withdrawal ending with
Huck sitting comfortably on Jackson's Island. Instead of a
hero's night of despair, the middle of the novel gives
us a relapse into easy living, conscious devotion to Jim,

and unconscious commitment to the King and the
Duke and the self-indulgence that they stand for.
The third stage of the quest, arising from latent attitudes
developed in the second one, is a new and better version of
the first—that is, the selfishness and self-indulgence
of the first, covered with a glow of the attractive
pseudo-commitment of the second.

One psychological satisfaction of the traditional
quest-action lies in seeing how the synthesis of the final
triumph arises logically from the thesis and antithesis of
earlier sections. The disgust felt by many while reading the
end of *Huckleberry Finn* arises from slowly realizing that
Twain is parodying this agreeable conclusion of the
quest-action, is doing so openly and unmercifully, and
is basing it all on the reader's blind voluntary commitment
to Huck earlier in the book. Most readers, I believe,
put up with the beginning while missing its lessons
and ignoring what it is committing them to. Most
readers—and the bulk of criticism bears this out—eagerly
accept the middle of the novel without seeing any tension
between the first part and Huck's behavior in the
middle, or between Huck's formal devotion to Jim and
his greater implicit interest in travel and excitement.
Thus, when Huck manages to have his cake and eat it
too, during the ending, a large number of readers, perhaps
the majority, feel betrayed. These readers are even
more outraged when Twain prolongs the evasion with
more and more absurd antics while depending upon
interest in Jim's fate to keep readers gritting their teeth and
plugging away through it all. And readers howl even
louder when they realize that this masochistic interest
in Jim is their own creation, not Huck's; in fact, the worst

blow of all is to realize that Huck thinks he is telling
our story too, that he is sure everyone wants to hear about
these exciting, irritating, wholly absorbing events,
and would have taken part in them if given the chance.
As we read, Huck makes us his accomplices. As we
recover and stand a little away from the book, we
realize that it is really Twain who has done that by standing
back and allowing us to make ourselves accomplices
from the opening sentence of the book. Twain thus makes
us show ourselves to ourselves, as human beings
dominated by the same unconscious cravings as the
characters', and as Americans dominated by our "drama"
of race. We cannot forgive him for making us make
fools of ourselves, and especially for making us see
ourselves.

II

In the reader's self-inflicted unified drama each
episode has its place. The general opinion of the opening
chapters is that they are desultory comedy, mildly
amusing at times but not going anywhere until Pap
kidnaps Huck. The reasoning seems to be that because these
scenes do not look important, they are not important.
There is a confusion here between seriousness and
solemnity. Comedy and farce, apparently, are not serious
art forms or ones that can contribute to the serious presentation
of a world-outlook in art. The ghost of Twain's enemy
Matthew Arnold raises its head to mutter, "How can the
antics of these tiresome boys create high seriousness?" If one
considers the opening, and especially the robber-gang
section, in isolation from the rest of the story, with the

belief that some conventionally uplifting meaning
ought to come of it all, and with the conviction that
anything else is "improvising," then he will agree with
De Voto that the opening has "no dynamic purpose."[7]

It is better to look at the novel in terms of what it does,
starting at the beginning. Twain's "Explanatory"
statement suggests that the novel has been written with
care. The "Notice" about motive, moral, and plot
suggests that the story does not have conventional
meanings, but does have some kind of meaning, probably
hidden. Both notes, especially the second one, suggest
the unconventional way in which meaning will come:
ironically, facetiously, outrageously. If we approach the
opening as something that gives us serious meanings
in a doubly improper way, we may get somewhere with it.
The critical error lies in seeing only the impropriety
and dismissing the whole thing as "merely comic" without
looking at it carefully and relating it to the rest of the
novel.

The first few chapters establish the world of the novel
and the characters in that world and in the action of
the novel. This seems quite enough to ask of one opening.
The first paragraph hints that we are going to be
given "truth" or truths, and by its rambling repetitious
style suggests that these truths will not be communicated
in a conventional way, and, further, that the world
to be presented is not conventional either. The
pointlessness of the opening chapters foreshadows the
rest of the book. There is no coherence in the world of
this St. Peterburg, unlike the same town in *The Adventures
of Tom Sawyer*. The characters do a great deal, but
accomplish nothing. They have the madly active

purposelessness of ants without the long-range order that
underlies ant behavior. Each of the characters is obsessed,
isolated in some desperate posturings that are desperate
dramatic responses to the desperate human situation.
Working with admirable economy, Twain gives us
the essence of the situation at once, at the end of chapter
1. After briefly exposing us to one of the maddest
characters, Miss Watson, and showing how she violates
others in playing out her Calvinist dramas, Twain presents
her disintegrating effects on Huck and the shaken
boy's glimpse of ultimate chaos. By the end of chapter 1
we know a good deal about human needs, human
awareness of those needs, and the kind of attempts men
make to satisfy those needs.

Or rather we experience this without realizing it.
We only realize it later when we look back and grasp the
pattern, which is presented several times in the opening
chapters. After Miss Watson comes a very different
character, harum-scarum Tom Sawyer, and after him a
character radically different from both, the slave Jim.
They are all alike, though. Each of the three characters
fulfills his need for temporal order, for drama, with
maximum energy and with total disregard for the
triviality of the materials at hand. Jim sticks to the
materials of his own low-status world, that is, to witchcraft
and superstition, but these are more than the trivia of
peasants; they are, as we eventually learn, the religion
of the novel. In the opening Twain not only raises
witchcraft to a serious matter; he reduces all human
behavior to the usual level of witchcraft, the level of trivia,
and then seriously shows how men take their trivia
seriously. It is the implication that everything is at once

trivial, silly, and important that an Arnoldian or
Emersonian critic cannot stand, because such an
implication violates the canons of both high seriousness
and democratic realism.

The opening also establishes the ground rules of this
manic world. From the judge's failure with Pap, and
Tom's failure with the gang, we learn that successful
drama-making requires not only desire and talent but also
the right situation, and the successful combination of
all three. With the boys in the cave we are given a
concentrated demonstration of how a leader, a dramatist,
establishes and maintains his leadership in the face
of criticism, illiteracy, and crises. That one crisis arises
from Huck's illiteracy and the other from a conspirator's
falling asleep should not deter readers from looking
through the surface to the essential meaning. From the
activities and failures of the gang we can derive the
aforementioned general rule that man will put up with a
great deal in order to gain dramatic satisfaction, but will
revolt if he feels his trust has been violated, and will
revolt the harder the more he has trusted. These laws
are relevant to the relations of Huck with the King and the
Duke, of the Wilks and Bricksville mobs with the
impostors, and most of all of Huck with Tom in the
conclusion. We also learn in the beginning the difference
between cultural agencies as passive dramatic props
(religion, reforming activities like the widow's and the
judge's) and cultural agencies as active teachers of drama.

In relation to teaching and learning drama, the
opening is a complete action, with a beginning, a middle,
and an end. It is Huck's education as a dramatist—
his search for dramatic power and his failure to find it.

The education begins with Huck's yielding to Tom's
demand that he go back to the widow's, that is, remain in
the world of others' dramas rather than retreat to his
private static world in the hogshead. Unable to develop
anything himself, driven half-crazy by Miss Watson's
aggressiveness yet attracted by the potentialities of
religion, irritated by Tom's bossiness but drawn by
his magnetism, Huck undergoes an agony in the opening
chapters. In the first hours of the novel he abandons
simple yea-saying American voluntarism because
he tries and fails to make himself cheerful (chap. 1). He
abandons more complex forms (magic) when he fails
to get anything out of verbal efforts (prayer) or physical
efforts (lamp-rubbing). Meanwhile other characters are
pursuing voluntarism and having difficulties that Huck
observes closely. Huck decides to go to hell, thus
abandoning the anchor of Christianity entirely; he yearns
only for change, and thus embarks on the endless
cycle of responses to situations that creates and controls
the underlying structure of the novel. He abandons
his freedom to Tom Sawyer, and although he finally
rejects Tom, he at once yields himself up to Pap, not
through fear, as a careful reading of chapter 5 shows, but
through interest. Pap fails Huck more than Tom does,
for Pap's first drama, his first great speech, casts
Huck merely as an observer, although he prefers active
roles; and Pap's second drama, his dt's, gives Huck an
unacceptable role, that of victim.

Unable to deal with any of these pressures—that is, inept
at gratuitous drama—Huck withdraws from the world,
"kills himself," and abandons himself to the drift of
the river. It is a modern, private catastrophe, not

destruction but self-destruction. The canoe in which he
lies is his new hogshead, and Jackson's Island is an
improved version of the tanyard. At this point the opening
of the novel ends. The power of situations, the
situation-changing mood cycle, and the need for drama—
these great principles of Huck's world, principles larger
than any personal need or quality, take over and generate
the middle of the book, leaving the beginning an entity.
The beginning also stands as the first part of the three-part
structure of the novel, running from the abandonment
of commitment, through the education in drama, to
the blending in the ending of intended moral commitment
to Jim and real dramatic commitment to Tom. Some
of the characteristics of the ending are suggested in the
beginning. The eager submission to Tom (chap. 2) closely
parallels the submission to Tom in the ending (chap. 34);
in each case it is capitulation not so much to Tom's
superior blarney, powerful though that is, as to the
reassurance that Tom's drama-making power gives Huck
after an attack of panic in the face of nature. In each case,
also, Tom appears, like a god (or a devil), at the moment
of greatest anxiety. And the Huck who says at the
beginning, under pressure from Miss Watson, "All I
wanted was to go somewheres; all I wanted was a change,
I warn't particular," is the Huck who, at the end,
reacts against the painful pressure of his obligation to
Jim and rushes off in every direction except the right one.

Twain fails to tell us why Miss Watson feels ashamed
at the idea of selling Jim down the river, but our
glimpses of her in the opening chapters allow a hypothesis
that fits the logic of the book and of Twain's fictionalized
southern world. The decision to free Jim, like the

earlier decision to sell him away from his family,
demonstrates her power to control people without
limit, and her urge to use that power. Like the slave-owner
Driscoll in *Pudd'nhead Wilson*, she enjoys playing God,
concealing sadism in thick layers of self-satisfying ritual.
We can see her drives openly in chapter 1, where she
forces Huck to sit still—that is, she deprives him of liberty
and in effect of life, for to a Twain boy liberty is life.
Deprived of Huck, Miss Watson turns on Jim, the other
available victim, and hurts him deeply while adhering
to the code of property and Presbyterian propriety. In the
situation of her deathbed she uses a traditional dramatic
model, the deathbed-repentance scene, to gain some
more credit; no other motive makes sense, because the
slave she is "freeing" has been gone for months and
can be presumed dead or safe up North. To the ignorant
public, though, she has sacrificed much and has made
herself a model of charity; but being dead, she loses
nothing—only her estate does. Miss Watson thus
achieves the ultimate capitalist triumph of getting
something for nothing. Also, she does have her quiet
triumph over Huck. He absorbs the didactic quality of
her lectures about the Bible even though he resists the
lectures themselves; and in chapter 14 he lectures
Jim about Solomon with Miss Watson's authoritarian
self-confidence but without her knowledge of the subject.

III

The middle of the novel, chapters 8–31, is Huck's return
to an education in the world. On the surface it seems to
involve Huck's commitment to Jim and his quest for

freedom for, and with, Jim. The interaction of surface theme and real theme produces complex ironies, which, like so much else in the novel, assert themselves indirectly and cumulatively, and produce an effect not of shock but of slowly growing uneasiness. The reader may accept missing the Ohio and wasting time at the Grangerfords, but after the King and the Duke take over and Huck seemingly forgets Jim, the reader may begin actively to demand the concentrated action of a "lyrical novel."[8] After these many chapters of evading the issue, the ending comes first as a relief—"Now it will happen!"—and then as the shock that makes readers howl. Thus Twain deviously makes the body of the novel serve the ending.

The early parts of the middle give glimpses of a satisfying romance. In chapter 1 Huck manifests a few characteristics of the typical romantic hero: his parents are not visible, he has no mother at all, and he has a treasure hoard. His turning to pastoral after his troubles with Pap is properly romantic.[9] But the lesson is clear as Huck, bored and restless, prowls the island and finds Jim: the romantic principle is subordinate here to the dramatic principle and is in fact relevant only in travesty (for example, Tom's mock-heroic arrival at the Phelpses and Tom's consistent use of romance in its trashiest form).

Huck's narrative method reinforces the presentation of the middle of the novel. Because Huck is practicing and learning all the time, both during the moment of experience and later during the time of writing, he narrates and describes in great detail and does so little himself that one critic has been led to complain that his passivity means the end of his "quest for freedom."[10]

Though it is clear that Huck is a secondary figure
in the middle of the novel, that fact would not necessarily
harm his quest (if he were on one) any more than the
virtual disappearance of the physical Ishmael in the middle
of *Moby-Dick* harms that novel (and, at any rate, I
see no evidence that Huck is on a quest). It is rather a
question of the author's strategies for getting his job done.
Considering Huck's role in the middle of the book, I
think that Huck, who chooses the material from his own
experience and writes the book, has disappeared not
from but into the narrative, so that every line of each
episode tells Huck something and tells us about Huck.
The Grangerford house reminds us of the pretentiousness
of the cotton snobs, but Huck's memories of it remind
him of experiences that he enjoyed and is eager to share.
The *Walter Scott* episode has strong overtones of
cultural satire for us, but for Huck it is (or was) practice
in *Sawyerismus* and a sharp lesson in the limits of
voluntarism and his own talents. Huck is not merely
imitating Tom Sawyer, as Richard Poirier sees it, in
these chapters before the Grangerford episode;[11] rather,
in order to do more than survive, Huck is trying to learn the
art of drama and is following the best practitioner he
knows. After Huck fails and falls back on attentive
observation of the dramas and dramatists before his eyes,
the references to Tom cease.

It is in the beginning of this middle section, the
Jackson's Island episode, rather than in chapter 31, that
Huck binds himself irrevocably to Jim. Like so much
else in the novel, and especially in the middle, this is done
with maximum indirection. When Jim says, "I owns
myself," and thus denies the basis of southern culture

in three words, Huck says nothing. As the reminiscing author-narrator, Huck places these words at the end of a chapter, thereby giving them added emphasis and finality. Huck's understatement here, or rather non-statement, is worth more than the "I'll go to hell" speech of chapter 31. By saying nothing Huck shows that he has already gone to "hell." Later he indicates his relationship to Jim by visiting Mrs. Loftus in disguise. In this rigid slave-holding culture any degree of ambivalence is defined as treason, and here Huck is doubly ambivalent, first as a "girl" concealing a boy, and then as "George Peters" concealing Huck Finn the slave-stealer. When Huck acts on Mrs. Loftus's information, he finally solidifies his illegal relationship to Jim and commits himself to a life of deceit (though he does not commit himself to activity on Jim's behalf).

In this episode also, Huck, having bound himself to Jim, betrays him and binds himself to evil, thus exactly foreshadowing the ending. Just after the flood all the animals are docile, there is a prolonged sense of peace, and nature proffers a union with man; this is the most intense part of the longest and strongest pastoral interlude in the book. But Huck violates the truce with man's old enemy the snake, kills a rattler, and puts it in Jim's bed as a joke. The snake's mate should revenge himself on Huck, but instead bites Jim. Huck's gratuitously evil act thus betrays nature, betrays Jim, and dooms both Jim and himself to a pattern of betrayal and failure in their own actions, their relations with other men, and their relations with nature. This is Huck's "original sin," and he never escapes it, as Jim predicts. The point is reinforced when Jack, Huck's servant

at the Grangerfords, leads Huck to "a whole stack o'
water-moccasins" (chap. 18), which turn out to be Jim.
The joy of Huck's and Jim's reunion is somewhat
dampened for the reader by the suggestion that Jim, like
the original snakeskin, is Huck's sin and Huck's burden.
The antics of the ending may be seen as hysterical
attempts to get shut of that snakeskin for good, but Huck
is shown that the opposite is happening—he and Tom
are opening Pandora's box—when the bag full of snakes is
opened and snakes swarm through the Phelps house.
The boys torture Jim with snakes, among other pets,
but underneath the fauna and all the rest Jim is still there,
still Huck's agonizing burden. The snake nonsense,
like the other antics of the boys, is designed not to
rescue Jim but to maximize the chances of getting him
killed.

The other central episodes likewise teach their lessons
in a roughly progressive way. There is a gradual
widening of significance from the Grangerfords through
the King's and the Duke's adventures and the Bricksville
horrors to the Wilks episode; and Huck gradually moves
closer to these events, as he goes from the complete
passivity and accidental involvement of the Grangerford
episode to energetic participation in the Wilks episode.
These central sections begin after Huck's bungling
of the *Walter Scott* business and the attempt to find
Cairo. His rather too obviously symbolic death and
rebirth, complete with deep immersion, wipe out his
failures and his worries about them. He is ready to observe
and to learn. From the point of view of Twain the writer,
the break, as Walter Blair has demonstrated, was a
way of avoiding the consequences of Huck's casual

commitment to Jim in chapter 8 and his impulsive saving of
Jim in chapter 16. Blair suggests that Twain quit
because he could not resolve the plot.[12] From my
consideration of the internal dynamics of the story, I
would say that Twain did not want to resolve it, that his
problem was not how to resolve it but how not to, or at
least how not to bring it up to the point where he would
need to face the results of what he had started in chapter 8
and brought out into the open in chapter 15. A man who
despised rigid behavior and who spent a good deal of
his life evading the consequences of commitments he had
made, Twain could not treat a character as close to him as
Huck was as if Huck were an ordinary fictional hero to be
run through a plot like that of *The Prince and the Pauper*.
Twain, in the 1870s at least, refused to do that with
Tom Sawyer. After the crisis with the slave-hunters in
chapter 15, Huck is so firmly committed to Jim that only a
deus ex machina like the steamboat can destroy the
momentum driving the plot toward—what? A cozy
steamboat ride up the Ohio and a triumphant return to
St. Petersburg, and Miss Watson, and, for all that
Huck knows, Pap? Or Jim's death, a grim conclusion
like the one thought up by Professor Seelye for *The True
Adventures of Huckleberry Finn*?

What Twain actually does is far more honest as a
projection of his own style and Huck's style. Having
committed himself to the good bourgeois life in his fabulous
house in Hartford, Twain dropped the whole thing four
years later (a year after dropping *Huck Finn*) and went to
Europe. Having saved Jim's life and risked his own
for him, Huck survives a disaster, forgets Jim utterly, and
enters a new life of relaxed and anti-dramatic behavior.

He is interested in the Grangerfords and their feud, he
enjoys living with them, but he does not argue vigorously
with them or share with them, as he did with Jim.
There are none of the strong reactions of the Wilks episode
or the spirited involvement of the ending. He completely
forgets to watch out for the Shepherdsons, and Buck
Grangerford is killed. Compare that with Huck's alertness
and quick thinking in several earlier episodes.

Also he fails, rather indifferently, with art. He does
not seem to care that he cannot figure out *Pilgrim's
Progress*. He does try to write some poetry as a tribute to
Emmeline Grangerford, but "I couldn't seem to make
it go, somehow" (chap. 17)—a sign of Huck's lack
of potency. His complex response to Emmeline suggests
his relation at this time and later to the Tom Sawyer
type of aggressive artist. Her strange, artificially
dramatic pictures "aggravate" Huck, and his admiration
for her poems is one of distant respect rather than
intuitive liking. Nevertheless he does admire the poems
and her headlong method of writing ("she would slap
down a line, and if she couldn't find anything to
rhyme with it she would just scratch it out and slap
down another one, and go ahead"), which resembles
Tom's method of impetuous improvisation: "I needn't
tell what [Tom's plan to steal Jim] was, here, because I
knowed it wouldn't stay the way it was. I knowed he
would be changing it around every which way, as we
went along, and heaving in new bullinesses wherever he
got a chance. And that is what he done" (chap. 34).
Huck admires Emmeline's youthful genius as he
later admires Tom's: "What a head for just a boy to
have!" (chap. 34).

Huck retains his dramatic potential, then, without
doing anything himself. The active, vigorous passages
involving Huck, like the sunrise passage in chapter 19, are
the product of Huck the writer after the fact, not of
Huck the participant at the time. The episodes with the
King and the Duke, however, bring Huck back into the
world of drama. Little by little the lesson is brought
home to him that even though situations often allow him
to evade participation, he ultimately cannot evade it. With
the King and the Duke life runs from falling in the river
to bullying, betraying, and lynching; Huck's reactions
run from laughter and amused contempt to fear and finally
to action against the frauds. It tells us something
rather ominous about Huck's (and Twain's) sense of
values that what finally moves Huck to such action is not
Jim's plight but the misery of a sweet young girl. A
major climax of a serious work on American race relations
is, alas, a sentimental attachment to a cliché of Victorian
kitsch.

Twain calls forth the Young Girl, the standard victim
of melodrama, because the King and the Duke have
become embodiments of aggressive evil, that is,
melodramatic villains. The two rascals also serve as
Dantean guides leading Huck to view man at his worst in
Bricksville, the static center of hell beyond which one
can go nowhere but up.[13] Bricksville is what Kroeber
called a cultural "climax," the focus of a cultural
area, where the values that form a culture appear in their
purest and strongest form.[14] Its climactic rottenness is
strengthened by its total isolation ("a little one-horse town
in a big bend"). Bricksville is the opposite of everything
that the word "Brick" meant for the Victorians of

Twain's generation: the strength and security of their
mansions and railroad depots and 7 percent gold bonds, the
loyalty and decency of a friend ("he's a brick"). The
town continues Huck's education by offering him the
book's most absurd dramatic failure (Boggs's attempt to
play badman) and its two most impressive dramatic
successes (the loafers' killing of time and the colonel's
killing of Boggs). No one in the town is doing anything in
the way of organized activities (the Grangerfords at
least toasted each other and went to church). Colonel
Sherburn himself is defined as leading citizen only
in terms of his clothes and his decorative, suspect title.
Bricksville is therefore the standard of anti-culture, or
rejection (of community and humanity) as a value and as a
basis for conduct.

The colonel's speech, apparently a model of rhetoric
and of advice for killers, is actually double-talk,
impressive gibberish, a verbal drama of pure "style"
comparable to the speech of Sister Hotchkiss (chap.
41). In the colonel's second paragraph, beginning
"Do I know you?", he implies that the "average [man]
all around" is a coward; then he differentiates the
individual northerner from the individual southerner, to
the advantage of the latter; then he repeats that
southerners are no braver than any other people; then
he says that juries (in the South) will not condemn a
murderer because his friends will assassinate the jurymen,
an action that we must assume will require courage.
What are we to make of this contradictory jumble? It
mesmerizes the mob, at any rate. In the colonel's second
paragraph the ideal man seems to be the one "who
stopped a stage full of men, in the day-time, and robbed the

lot"; in the third paragraph the ideal is the man who "goes in the night, with a hundred masked cowards at his back" and murders someone. Who is better, the lone-wolf daytime robber or the sociable nighttime lyncher? Sherburn does not say, and of course Huck does not. In the last paragraph of his speech the colonel says, "If any real lynching's going to be done, it will be done in the dark, Southern fashion." This is virtually an invitation to the mob, but nothing comes of it—as far as we know. In this confused and confusing speech is Twain attacking mobs, or praising the frontier badman (already a legend by 1880)? Whatever Twain's aims, the speech, like so much else in *Huckleberry Finn*, shows how dramatic intensity can make nonsense real and the real nonsense when there are no standards of reference, no "bricks," to appeal to. The speech is Sherburn's gesture of contempt for logic and a reminder of what the colonel's weapons, very American weapons, really are—charisma and a shotgun.

The moral of all this is wasted on Huck, who is apparently impressed by the colonel's "style," but remains withdrawn from action and evaluation until the Wilks episode. This section is the longest in the book before the ending, but it has been largely neglected, or attacked.[15] Its length, given Huck's interest in truth-telling, should suggest that it is important to Huck. As the most highly plotted episode, it should attract admirers of form and complexity, but readers are put off by its literariness— the outlandish coincidences, the sentimentality, the use of melodramatic types. From the point of view of Huck and his education, however, this melodramatic atmosphere is admirable. Here is a world of pure drama, for

melodrama is "the quintessence of drama."[16] This
world is like the Grangerfords' world but more fluid and
therefore more open to an outsider like Huck. At the
Grangerfords he could accelerate the denouement but not
change it. Now, for the first time, Huck can take
part in a manageable gratuitous drama, one that lasts
for a while (unlike the frantic survival dramas in the early
episodes), one that puts him in a position where he can
accomplish something without being overmatched.
This drama is quite different from Huck's own desperate
survival dramas, or the two rascals' hoaxes that Huck
observes as a docile underling. The dramatic training has
important implications for the ending, where Huck
applies his experience for his own ends.

    This is not to say that Huck does well either as a valet or
as a counter-conspirator. When put to the test by Joanna
Wilks, Huck fails miserably. De Voto sees this as an
inconsistency, Huck having no trouble making up stories
elsewhere,[17] but the situation is special here. Huck either
does not like or does not know the people he lies to elsewhere,
but he does like the Wilks girls. Anyway, the incident
is not his own survival drama; telling a good story to
Joanna will not get Huck anywhere, in more than one
sense. The episode thus provides Huck with practice
in fooling people he likes, and in the conclusion he
makes good use of this experience. Huck also learns that
he is poor at such fooling, and later he leaves the
bamboozling of the Phelpses to Tom. Most of all, Huck in
the Wilks episode is able to study dramatic failure at
close range. The already advanced state of his dramatic
education is suggested by the intensity of his disgust at the
King's slovenly acting of a preacher's role. As the

episode continues, Huck sees what happens when men highly competent at short simple dramas take on long complex ones. Huck's effort to help Mary Jane Wilks is a gauge of his exasperation at the "beats" as well as his admiration for Miss Watson's antithesis, the true heroine of the novel. The final touch is the snarling return of the King and the Duke when Huck is sure he has escaped at last. All this makes Huck eager not only to escape the frauds but to accept a really competent dramatist when one comes along. By the end of the Wilks episode Huck has graduated from his school of drama and is ready for Tom Sawyer again.

IV

But first Huck goes through the crisis of chapter 31, probably the most discussed and the most admired episode in *Huckleberry Finn*. It is here that Huck formally defies his culture, decides to go to hell rather than turn Jim in, and sets out to steal him. Most readers consider this decision the crisis of the novel and Huck's action an admirable denunciation of his society. The analysis of Henry Nash Smith develops the thesis that Huck moves from false conventional responses, expressed in the false official language of the novel, to honest personal responses, expressed in true vernacular.[18] I see chapter 31 rather differently, as a drama that resembles the others in the novel more than it differs from them, and as an episode that, depending on future situations, may or may not lead to any given conclusion. I will examine this chapter in terms of its relation to the logic of the world of the novel, its structure, its language, and its significance.

There is no reason to see chapter 31 as a climax to be
followed by a certain conclusion. A critic who approaches
the novel as picaresque might find it desirable to drop
the idea of a conclusion, or at least to drop the idea that any
one episode is the cause of the conclusion. For picaresque
W. B. Gallie has proposed the useful term "interim
conclusions": "We could . . . if we wished,
speak of following a story through a series of interim
conclusions to a final conclusion."[19] Because *Huckleberry
Finn* is situational and sequential, with episodes
developing out of the principles of drama, it is an error to
isolate a "conclusion" as final or the cause of a final
conclusion; it is better to consider all the "interim
conclusions" and evaluate the final one in terms of them
all. This is what I do below in trying to justify the ending of
Huck Finn. We should think of chapter 31 in the light
of what goes before. As I have said, Huck's real
commitment to Jim, as far as society is concerned, comes
in chapter 8 when he fails to comment on Jim's subversive
statement, "I owns myself." The commitment may be
put a little earlier, when Huck fails to report Jim as soon as
he sees him asleep—after all, what other reason than
escape could Jim have for being on that island? The
commitment is tightened with every mile the raft floats
down the river into the Deep South. Certainly it is
tightened as far as his culture is concerned. Huck may be
untroubled by his situation, and often acts as if it did not
exist, but in this culture there are no halfway covenants
where slavery is concerned. The Grangerford episode
in many ways foreshadows chapter 31 and decreases its
effect. Huck loses Jim, learns that he is in a "prison" (in
the depths of a swamp), ignores him for what might be

an indefinite time, finally is reunited with him (by
necessity, not choice), and then continues the raft journey.
After all that, why should another spell of imprisonment
for Jim and another adventure for Huck spell the end of
the journey? To be sure, Twain decided to end it there, but
he did not need to. He could have omitted Tom
Sawyer; he could have had Huck break into the cabin, slip
the chain off the bed-leg, and walk off with Jim toward
another adventure or adventures. Chapter 31 is, then, not a
bombshell; it is one episode.

If one considers the novel as the story of Huck's
moral rise, then chapter 31 makes a good climax. But the
wheel that raises Huck to his peak must continue to
turn and bring him down. Huck has his moment of
epiphany, his union with nature and the moral world; but
that moment can only be a moment, one situation in
a succession of situations. If it were not, then the whole
novel would be a comedy, not a popular word among critics
of the novel. It is better to admit the ending, accept
that Huck's moment of "life" in chapter 31 is followed by a
"death" in chapter 32 and a rebirth as, of all things,
Tom Sawyer. The novel then becomes tragicomedy, a more
modern form than tragedy or comedy and one more
suited to the genre of the novel.

The episode is reverie, and it can be attacked as
unsatisfactory reverie in terms of the "rules" established in
the course of the novel, which is by now thirty chapters
and about two hundred pages long. The reverie is
acceptable in itself, for Huck has done a good deal of
brooding during his many hours of solitude. The situation is
fitting for reverie: Huck is disgusted, and he is alone.
The first thoughts about social pressures are acute. Miss

Watson *is* the kind of woman who would sell Jim again
out of spite, and the town *would* despise Huck for stealing a
slave. He knows himself, too: "It would get all around,
that Huck Finn helped a nigger to get his freedom; and if I
was to ever see anybody from that town again, I'd be
ready to get down and lick his boots for shame." This is a
"shame culture," in which people act according to
what others will think (if the others find out and if their
opinions matter), as much as a "guilt culture," in which
people act according to internalized principles. We
have known that since the fifth paragraph of the novel,
where the widow attacks smoking, although "she took
snuff . . . ; of course that was all right, because she
done it herself" (chap. 1).

But from cultural analysis Huck turns to brooding
about his conscience and what he should have learned but
did not learn at Sunday school, and with this the
episode falls down. "The more I studied about this the
more my conscience went to grinding me"—why? The
transition is handled smoothly, but it is Twain doing the
manipulating, not Huck moving from one topic to another
according to the laws developed in the book. What
happens here is the return, under stress, of Huck's
obsession with conscience. This obsession is the extension
of Twain's own.[20] Huck could not acquire a conscience
from the members of the book's culture; they do
not have consciences. Some of them have great native
kindness, but the irrelevance of that to conscience is well
revealed in the famous exchange between Huck and
Aunt Sally, the most sweet and motherly character in the
book:

> "We blowed out a cylinder-head."
> "Good gracious! Anybody hurt?"

"No'm. Killed a nigger."
"Well, it's lucky; because sometimes people do get hurt."
(Chap. 32)

The novel demonstrates the lack of conscience. Huck's
irritation with it has a rough relevance, because
conscience is an organizing, synthesizing principle, and
Huck tries to avoid constants and fixity. The active,
turbulent world of this novel cannot contain conscience; it
is entirely irrelevant.

It may be irrelevant, but it is still taught, in Sunday
schools and elsewhere, as surface culture. Huck is right in
saying he *could* have learned it at Sunday school. But
consider the way in which the point is presented:
"Something inside of me kept saying, 'There was the
Sunday-school, you could a gone to it; and if you'd a done it
they'd a learnt you, there, that people that acts as I'd been
acting about that nigger goes to everlasting fire.' " This
will not do. It suggests that Huck does not know what
he says he knows. We have a boy judging himself according
to principles that he admits he does not know. He is
talking about "something inside of me" that "kept
saying"—that is, he is referring to ground-in knowledge,
what Twain in *What Is Man?* was to refer to as "training,"
in opposition to mere knowing-about (Twain, as a patient
student of the German language, was aware of the
distinction between *wissen* and *kennen*). In the opening
chapters Huck rejects a stock indoctrination into
conventional Christian morality, rejects it on firmly
pragmatic grounds, and acts toward it as if it were all a
complete novelty to him. No moral voice "inside of me"
develops in the opening; the authentic voice of those
chapters is the one of Huck's real experience, the one that
says, "I don't take no stock in it." And certainly Huck

does not develop a conscience as he goes through
the novel—he has no chance to.

If Huck does learn anything in the opening, he learns to
hate cant. His experiences in the rest of the book
reinforce that. Certainly in the Wilks episode his loathing
for the King's cant is close to nausea. But in chapter 31
cant, the public language that Henry Nash Smith has well
defined,[21] starts flowing spontaneously into Huck's
mind, and he starts to admire it and to admire himself for
thinking it. This will not do either; it is false to Huck's
character and to the novel.[22] It is true that Huck is made to
speak a certain kind of public language in earlier scenes
in which he is troubled by his terrible crime against his
culture. He thinks, for example, "Here was this nigger
which I had as good as helped to run away, coming right
out flat-footed and saying he would steal his children—
children that belonged to a man I didn't even know; a man
that hadn't ever done me no harm" (chap. 16). For
Huck this is the right kind of cant, the cant of general
cultural values that are taught and learned without benefit
of Sunday school and that need no formal learning
because they are part of the atmosphere that people
(whites) breathe from birth. When Huck mentions his
"conscience" in that scene from chapter 16, he is
using the term correctly in terms of the world of the book—
that is, he is using it with unconscious irony to refer to
the internalized values of his culture and the psychological
mechanisms that make those values effective. In chapter
31, however, Twain makes him use "conscience"
incorrectly.

Finally Huck says, "All right, then, I'll *go* to hell,"
and tears up that letter to Miss Watson. The first action is

verbal; the second one is negative (not-sending). Neither
commits him irrevocably to anything new—Huck opts
for hell in the sixth paragraph of the book, and destroying
the letter leaves him no more and no less a "nigger-stealer"
than he has been since he ran across Jim in the woods on
Jackson's Island. Not turning in a slave is, to be sure,
something of an achievement in a culture as rigid and as
passionately founded on one issue (slavery) as this culture.
It is, nevertheless, a major achievement only if one
believes that not doing something is a major achievement, if
one believes that conscious commitment in chapter 31 is
more important than behavior in chapter 8, and, most
of all, if one can still believe, after thirty chapters, that
conscious commitment rather than behavior is really
meaningful in the world of *Huckleberry Finn*. Many
intellectuals, being verbal types anyway, assume that
pronouncements are real actions rather than symbolic
actions, and overlook Twain's book-long demonstration
that language is not itself reality but a device for dealing
with reality.

It helps to see chapter 31 not as gospel but as a record put
down with no grasp of what it means (and, from Twain's
side, without much attention to the decorum of point
of view). Then, it itself, it becomes a drama, a dramatic
monologue, that tells us more than the speaker realizes or
wishes us to know, in contrast to a soliloquy, in which
the speaker is objective about himself and the world.[23] On
the surface Huck's reverie is a noble melodrama of
self-sacrifice and renunciation. Beneath that it tells us that
Huck has had a glimpse of better things, a high level of
perceiving and living, but that in a situational world the
glimpse is only momentary. Ignoring wider implications, I

148

think that the scene suggests the theory of motivation
articulated in *What Is Man?*: "A man often honestly *thinks*
he is sacrificing himself merely and solely for some one
else, but he is deceived; his bottom impulse is to
content a requirement of his nature and training, and thus
acquire peace for his soul."[24] Huck does attain peace
in this episode, first by writing the letter and then by
tearing it up and accepting a punishment ("going to hell")
that he really does not mind. Earlier in the book he
justifies his habitual thefts of food by giving up one fruit
that is not ripe yet and one fruit that he dislikes. In
chapter 31 he is the same Huck; but the situation has
changed, and now his sophistical use of gestures is not
funny.

At the end of chapter 31 we can predict nothing with
certainty; we know only that something will happen,
because something always does happen in the turbulent
world of this novel. If we place the episode in the context
of the whole book it makes sense and fits with the
ending—Huck never does write to Miss Watson, he does
rescue Jim, and he risks both social and physical hell
in doing so. In this sense chapter 31 is profoundly ironic,
suggesting the unlimited gap between man's sincere
pretenses and his actual behavior, and also profoundly true
to a world where men are dominated by situations and by
the need to dramatize those situations.

1. Twain tried to use Huck in the unfinished "prairie-manuscript,"
and did use him in *Tom Sawyer Detective* and *Tom Sawyer Abroad*, neither
of which add any dimensions to Huck or indeed have much literary
quality. The prairie-manuscript has been edited by Walter Blair and

published in *Life*, 20 December 1968, pp. 32A–50A, and in *Hannibal, Huck, and Tom* (Berkeley: University of California Press, 1969), pp. 81–140. Blair thinks that Twain dropped the story because he was unable to deal with a rape to which his narrative had become committed. But the story was going nowhere, and if it had had any vitality, Twain's fertile mind would never have been utterly defeated by a narrative block of the sort Blair discusses.

2. *Harper's Weekly* 41 (13 February 1897): 155. Howells was reviewing the first five volumes of Harper's Uniform Edition of Twain's works. Note Howells's respectful discussion of "romance" in *Criticism and Fiction*.

3. A. A. Mendilow, *Time and the Novel* (London: Peter Nevill, 1952), pp. 106 ff.

4. *The Rhetoric of Fiction* (Chicago: University of Chicago Press, 1961), pp. 187 ff.

5. Northrop Frye comments devastatingly on this point in *The Well-Tempered Critic* (Bloomington: Indiana University Press, 1963), pp. 17 ff.

6. See "The Enchanted Sea-Wilderness" and "The Great Dark" in John S. Tuckey, ed., *Mark Twain's "Which Was the Dream?"* (Berkeley and Los Angeles: University of California Press, 1967), pp. 76–88, 102–50.

7. *Mark Twain at Work*, p. 54. A more favorable analysis is in Poirier's *A World Elsewhere*, pp. 179–91.

8. Robert Murray Davis, ed., *The Novel: Modern Essays in Criticism* (Englewood Cliffs, N.J.: Prentice-Hall, 1969), pp. 66–67.

9. *Anatomy of Criticism*, pp. 198, 199 ff.

10. *Mark Twain: The Development of a Writer*, pp. 116–17.

11. *A World Elsewhere*, pp. 189 ff.

12. *Mark Twain and Huck Finn*, pp. 145–51.

13. See Northrop Frye's discussion of the last stage of satire in *Anatomy of Criticism*, pp. 238–39.

14. Abram Kardiner and Edward Preble, eds., *They Studied Man* (New York: New American Library, 1963), p. 168.

15. A typical, and typically brief, attack is in De Voto's *Mark Twain's America*, p. 312.

16. Eric Bentley, *The Life of the Drama*, p. 216.

17. *Mark Twain's America*, p. 312.

18. *Mark Twain: The Development of a Writer*, pp. 120–23.

19. *Philosophy and the Historical Understanding*, p. 27.

20. Twain's concern with conscience is dramatized in "The Recent Carnival of Crime in Connecticut" (1876) and discussed in *Mark Twain and Huck Finn*, chap. 10.

21. *Mark Twain: The Development of a Writer*, pp. 121–23.

22. J. R. Boggan notes Twain's error in "That Slap, Huck, Did It Hurt?", *English Language Notes* 1 (March 1964): 212–15.

23. Robert Langbaum, *The Poetry of Experience: The Dramatic Monologue in the Modern Literary Tradition* (New York: Random House, 1957), p. 146.

24. *What Is Man?*, p. 140.

The Dramatic Unity of *Huckleberry Finn*

The Outrageous Logic of the Ending

I

For Bernard De Voto, one of the first modern critics to
take Twain seriously, the ending of *Huckleberry Finn* was
a deep disappointment, "inharmonious burlesque,"
"a separate episode, unrelated to the rest, self-contained
but improvised"[1]—an opinion shared by a great many critics
and readers. I hold that the ending is just the opposite.
It follows the rule that Twain himself later postulated:
"There is only one right form for a story, and if you fail to
find that form the story will not tell itself."[2] The one right
form for the ending of *Huckleberry Finn* is a final
devastating demonstration of the principles developed
earlier in the novel: the power of situation, the need for
reciprocal activity, the need for dramatic organizing
of situations. The ending is such a demonstration. Only a
child or a sadist, I repeat, could find elements of such
an ending thoroughly enjoyable; but *Huckleberry Finn* is
serious art, not entertainment, and the question of

conventional enjoyment is, in the last analysis, irrelevant.
At any rate, who can deny that in some ways it is a
happy ending? Huck and Tom get as much as they could
expect from a given situation, and Jim gets what he
must have, his freedom.

In the following pages, then, I will be trying to show that
the ending is meaningful burlesque, is not a separate
episode, and is related to the rest of the novel. The
relations of Tom and Huck, which I will deal with in some
detail, are, to be sure, preposterous on the surface, but
they are logical in terms of the hidden laws of relationships
developed throughout the novel and suggested in the
terms "reciprocity" and "deep structure." The hidden laws
of situationalism apply: good resolutions and verbal
formulas give way to the demands of Huck's situation and
the need for drama. Events that are crazy and chaotic
in themselves are orderly when seen in the light of
the hidden structures of emotional response and drama.
There is continuity of technique and tone. Twain fulfills his
prefatory brag about his mastery of southwestern dialect.
The bizarre, sometimes magical, sometimes sinister
tone of the ending concentrates and intensifies qualities
found elsewhere in the novel. Twain boxes us in here
the way he boxed us in with Huck in the widow's parlor,
Pap's cabin, and the Wilks house. The ending is serious
work. Though Twain had little in common with Henry
James, he managed in this ending to obey James's
warning that an author must control the "stream" of
improvisation lest it become a "flood" and lose "the great
effect . . . of keeping on terms with itself."[3]

The ending, whether carelessly improvised or not, has
been seen as a distortion of what goes before. As a

neutral description, the term is correct. If one uses the word
"distortion," as Ronald Paulson uses it, to mean the twist
of a common literary form to convey a satiric message,
then *Huckleberry Finn* takes its place as a modern novel.[4]
One of Frank Kermode's most acute observations is that
modern literature denies apocalypse, the final ending of an
action.[5] By rejecting stasis or any clear permanent change
for Huck, Twain makes *Huckleberry Finn* a modern work,
an account of an eternal transition, toward what we do
not know.[6] Such an ending is for Kermode the triumph of
"common sense" over "free imagination," which
panders in conventional fiction to the reader's urge for
"fantasy gratification." A really modern novel, according
to Kermode, disappoints one's "schematic expectations"[7]
at the very beginning; but because this expectation is
founded on the tradition of peripeteia, *Huckleberry Finn*
manages very well by apparently offering a turning point in
chapter 31 and then withdrawing it. Twain here is more
modern and more honest than his great contemporary
George Eliot, who twists the end of *The Mill on the Floss* to
make it a conventional novel: "The novel refuses the
prose realities, and saves its heroine from the pains of fresh
starts and conflicts by invoking the very narrative
consolations it has been concerned to analyze and deny."[8]
Twain avoids "narrative consolations"—there is no
dispute about that. The novel is full of premonitions of
disaster; the ending is that disaster. Though not a
true picaresque, *Huckleberry Finn* moves, as picaresque
does, "not toward a happy ending or moral wholeness,
but toward strictly prudential knowledge."[9] The end
of *Huckleberry Finn* succeeds, I believe, because it gives us
that kind of knowledge; that is, it demonstrates the

dismaying nature of man and his world as Twain saw them
and reaffirms the dismaying demonstrations of the earlier
chapters. By doing that and by denying the consolations
of a pleasant ending, the ending for which most readers
and critics yearn, Twain outrages them.

II

Although not emotionally consoling, the ending is
logically consoling. Its differences from the earlier sections
are less in kind than in degree. Like the beginning and the
middle, the ending is a demonstration of human qualities
and the world in which they exist; the differences lie
in the situation, which makes Tom Sawyer unpleasantly
visible and puts the burden of the demonstration on
Huck, in a way that most readers find unpleasant too. It
is easy to make Tom look bad—the cave scene (chap. 2)
alone suffices to reveal his noisy aggressiveness—but it takes
most of a book to prepare a situation in which Huck can
be made to look bad. The incidents are much the same
in the beginning and in the ending, but our reactions to
them are different—a tribute to Twain's handling of
the middle sections. In their wildness the incidents of the
ending join in a series beginning with the tricking of Jim in
chapter 2. Now, though, Twain makes us question that
wildness. In chapter 1 Huck gets Tom when he needs him;
in the ending Huck gets Tom twice, so to speak: he
becomes Tom, and he meets him again. But rather than
applaud Huck's double luck, or take the whole matter
indifferently (as most readers take the early chapters), we
are troubled by that luck, because between chapters 1
and 32 we have learned something about Huck's world and
the consequences of acting like Tom Sawyer. Tom's

dramas at beginning and end resemble each other
remarkably: each is unreal, highly contrived, and basically
riskless for Tom, and each runs afoul of authority
(represented by the Sunday-school teacher and the posse).
These similarities draw one's attention to the differences
that give the ending its point: a Sunday-school teacher
yelling is hardly comparable to a posse shooting, and
pestering children is not the same as playing with a man's
life.

On the level of detail the similarities of the two sections
reinforce differences in meaning. The arguments of the
boys over the sleeping Jim and in the cave are almost
identical to those during the ending. Tom wins in both
cases; but in the ending Huck should win, and it matters
that he does not. In chapter 2 it is funny that Huck should
worry more about his itching nose than about Jim's
reaction to being tricked; in the last chapters Huck's
self-centeredness and indifference to Jim are not funny at
all. We applaud Huck when he quits Tom's gang because
there is no "profit" in it, and we assume that Huck
is through with "profit," psychological satisfaction, as he
was with prayer; but in the conclusion Huck pursues
"profit" as if he had been hungry for it all along. We are
driven to realize that this is true of Huck as it is of any
man; we acquire "prudential knowledge" about the unity of
the damned human race.

Other incidents bind the ending to the early episodes
of the book. Though Huck fears Pap, he is Pap's son and
listens without comment to Pap's familiar anarchist
diatribes. Even if Huck's slave-stealing reflects Pap's hatred
of the propertied classes in terms of action rather than
attitude, Huck is nevertheless fulfilling Pap's intention.

Huck's absorbed activity during the early part of the ending
(chaps. 34–38) suggests his controlled intensity during
his own escape from a cabin (in chap. 7), with the
difference that the later example seems "pointless" to the
observer of the surfaces of the novel, and that Tom, wished
for in vain before, is very much present throughout the
ending. The simplicity and similarity of the two
imprisonments throw a glaring light on the complexities
of the ending. If the problem is simply to get a person out of
a cabin, why cannot Huck just do it? He did it once, with
ease. Like so much else in, or suggested by, the ending,
such a question serves to bring us back to the central
problems of the novel.

The center of the novel has fewer links to the conclusion,
as befits a circular structure in which beginning and end
are closely related. The end does continue from the
middle, though. When Huck abandons Jim for the fun with
Tom, we should recall that he did much the same thing
at the Grangerfords and did it again at the Wilkses, and
that however little he does for Jim during the evasion, he
does nothing at all for him in the other two cases and
is actively cruel to him elsewhere. Huck's submission to
Tom at the end is not as complete as his earlier submission
to Buck and the feud. Buck is proud that the feud has
gone on for years and will go on indefinitely, as it would
but for Huck. Tom hopes to keep up the evasion so it will
involve the next generation and last "as much as eighty
year" (chap. 36)—an ambition no greater than Buck's.
Huck's repeated references to Tom and his "style" (chaps.
7, 12, 28) make us keep in mind his appetite for drama.
The King and the Duke reinforce it. Just before the evasion
the Wilks episode gives Huck a taste of the pleasure of

acting, and adds lessons in scheming, risking the truth, trusting to Providence, and driving hubristically beyond limits. Huck is thoroughly ready for the ending that Twain gives him.

Like the links to earlier parts of the novel, the internal qualities of the ending serve to reinforce and reemphasize Twain's meanings. The length of the ending suggests its importance, especially for Huck. For the first time in the book Huck is completely secure and relaxed, and, despite his pledges to Jim, he is going to enjoy himself; for he is, we are constrained to see, an easygoing white boy first of all and the dedicated friend of the black slave Jim second. "There ain't no hurry; le's keep on looking around," says Tom (chap. 34); and Huck, as he often does, acquiesces silently. During the ending Twain also is in no hurry. He has arrived at the point in his book where he can, and indeed must, work out his ideas, and use the world and the implications that he has built up during thirty-odd chapters of fiction. Even if Huck is not exactly where he aimed to be when he set out, Twain is—right in the middle of the respectable middle classes, where he can examine "man," the people who count and who counted for him, on a large scale in relation to a controlling cultural drama (slavery) and on a small scale in their responses to a gratuitous drama (the evasion) experienced from beginning to end. The agonizing length of the evasion further rubs in a moral that Twain has been suggesting through the book: the best gratuitous drama is the longest. (For obvious reasons, survival dramas should be short.) The length of the evasion is internally determined only by an intrusion of reality (the Phelpses sending out notices about Jim) that Tom cannot control.

Sticking closely to this pattern, Twain avoids
complexities that his fabled love of "improvising" might
have led him into. He passes up the interesting approach,
suggested by Sister Hotchkiss, of having the slaves help
Jim, either surreptitiously or by raising a rebellion. By
including Tom Sawyer, Twain solves the problem of
developing Huck's common and inferior qualities in a
situation that would tend to make Huck heroic and
impressive, the Cooperesque situation of the lone wolf
fighting to save his friends from a horde of enemies.
(Professor Seelye, in his rewritten version of the novel,
gains added sympathy for Huck by keeping him solitary.) If
Tom's presence is acceptable, the problem then is to get
him back into the story at this point. Avoiding elaborate
maneuvers ("improvisations"), Twain assaults the
problem head on, suggesting that he knows what he wants
to do and wants to get at it, however crudely.

It is coincidence that Tom has relatives in Arkansas, that
they are the ones who take Jim, that Tom is visiting
at just that time, and that Huck meets Tom on the road to
town. We are now in a different world, a world of
coincidences and rigged symbolic situations, a world of
romance. If Bricksville is hell on earth in terms of human
behavior, the Phelps farm is hell on earth in terms of
imagery. Fox fire, witches, witch-pie, nighttime
skulduggery, a tireless charismatic leader of the revels in
Tom Sawyer: we are in a demonic world. The slave
Nat is right—the dogs that bulge in under Jim's bed *are*
witches. If Nat were more analytical, he would realize that
Tom's domination of the dogs makes him the chief
witch and thus a version of Satan. The insanely pointless
digging, the rapid sequence of absurd and irrelevant

activities, the steady speeding-up of the pace—all this
creates the effect, characteristic of demonic imagery,
of being trapped in a maze designed by ingenious sadists.[10]
When Twain tries to emphasize the wildness of the
chaos, the turbulence, he characteristically overdoes it,
and piles on scenes like the episode of the rats and snakes
that escape the boys and overrun the house. Yet even
the hysterical humor of this episode has a certain logical
significance; a gratuitous drama like this one, left free to
shape itself, inevitably escapes, overruns its makers,
and winds up imitating the chaos it was designed to order.
Twain caps this effect, and redeems any errors he has
made, in the final presentation of the interior of
Jim's cabin as seen through the eyes of the Phelpses'
drama-hungry neighbors. Here is pure chaos, experienced,
reported, discussed, and turned into legend, the most
durable form of drama.

The boys add to the chaos by their behavior, which is
"goofy," in the sense that Nabokov uses the word in
Lolita to describe a self-centered, disorganized, ignorant,
gum-chewing, comic-book-reading American adolescent of
the 1950s. Just as Lolita fails to rise to Humbert Humbert's
lofty ideal of love, the boys fail to rise to the reader's
lofty ideal of loyalty to Jim. To us, the ending is
melodrama, unwanted and exasperating; to Tom Sawyer,
a privileged and arrogant child, a kind of male nymphet,
the ending is farce; for he cannot see, and at any rate
cannot suffer from, the element of danger that turns
farce into melodrama. Because Huck, like any child, does
not think of himself and his friends as children, we
tend to forget that Huck and Tom *are* children, or no more
than the kind of early adolescents who lapse easily from

their adult pose into childish behavior, goofiness. One
function of the ending is to restore us from romance to the
level of "prudential knowledge," or, in simple terms, to
remind us of the consequences of sending a boy to do a
man's job. Some of the foolishness is Huck's, and
follows from his inability to make up stories outside a
narrow range (imaginary family troubles). When he tries to
conceal his visit to the cellar (chap. 40) or the reason
for his prolonged absence from the Phelps house (chap. 41),
he flubs the job, with comic results.

The goofiness is actually functional, though, to a
cultural treatment of the material. Huck is at last sharing
in the harmony of a culture; his isolation, dissatisfaction,
anxiety, and harassments are over, after more than
thirty chapters. Because he is a boy, his assigned role in
the Phelps household is that of a harum-scarum prankster,
and he plays it well. This may be intensely irritating to
a reader who assumes that Huck exists for the sake of Jim,
but it is all highly satisfying for Huck. He lives through
it all naturally (that is, according to the laws of his culture)
and reports it all to us in a tranquil spirit. Thus when he
and Tom tell Jim they will not free him right away
and Jim says it is "all right," Huck says nothing and later
reports the conversation without comment. At the time
Huck is not aware of Jim's feelings, his pathetic
dependence on the boys and his need to keep control of
himself in this desperate situation. Neither is Huck aware
later, when he writes the book. A sensitive adult
narrator could make much out of that quiet "all right."
The novel is epitomized by Huck's failure to do so.

This goofiness has its ironic side. It is not entirely
childish or adolescent. Huck can fail to understand Jim
during the evasion and still fail to understand him during

the writing of the book, because Huck is for the first
time acting as a *man*, in full harmony with the laws of his
world. He acts mature; but because adults in this world
act like foolish children when they can, Huck now acts like
a foolish child. Earlier he had to act like a model Victorian
adult: shrewd, prudent, reserved. Now Huck is not
merely observing dramas blankly, or judging them out of
hard-earned knowledge; he is acting them out himself
and making a real impact on people and events. Even if the
details of the evasion are Tom's, the basic idea—stealing
Jim—is Huck's, and some of the key touches are his. A
natural end for an autobiographical narrative comes when
the author-narrator "comes to terms with himself,
assumes his vocation."[11] Huck never consciously
understands his nature, of course, because he is insensitive
to it, and his world does not stimulate him to introspection;
but he is nevertheless assuming his vocation, which
in the simple vision that Twain is projecting means less
that he is a certain kind of man than that he is simply a
man. And when a youth assumes manhood and enters upon
his vocation, he preserves a certain distance toward
outsiders. Even when he is helping Jim, Huck must do so at
a formal distance; for Jim is now an outsider, an object
in a drama rather than a participant in it. Thus the apparent
indifference toward Jim. Gone are the leisurely
arguments and intimate silences of the raft voyage, when
Huck, too, was an object in dramas rather than an
instigator of them and participant in them. Huck's
contentment is now with the Phelps family, and his role as
indulged nephew feeds his goofiness.

III

    At the beginning of the final episode none of these

general truths are apparent. We can become aware of them
only after experiencing the ending as a series of scenes and
statements. The ending has been attacked on this level
as an incoherent jumble. Here if anywhere De Voto's
accusation of "improvising" is relevant, and here I must
face the accusation that the progress of the episode not only
is illogical in itself but destroys the promise inherent
in chapter 31. My thesis is that chapter 31, despite its
internal flaws, has a logical if ironical relation, in terms of
Twain's view of things, to the last chapters, and that
these chapters are an orderly progression of incidents
arising from the relations of the characters and the laws of
the world of the novel.

In *What Is Man?*, which so often expresses what the
earlier works imply, Twain's spokesman says, "The fact
that man knows right from wrong proves his *intellectual*
superiority to the other creatures; but the fact that he can
do wrong proves his *moral* inferiority to any creature that
cannot."[12] Chapter 31 of *Huckleberry Finn* illustrates the
first part of this statement; the last chapters illustrate the
second part. As Ovid more elegantly phrased it, "Video
meliora proboque, deteriora sequor." In relation to
chapter 31 the ending shows us what Twain says to us in
What Is Man?: "[Will] has nothing to do with *intellectual
perception of right and wrong*, and is not under their
command" (p. 201). When Huck says, "All right, I'll go
to hell," he sincerely wills the idea, but he does not know
the difference between willing and acting. His creator,
though, demonstrates in the ending the importance of that
bit of "prudential knowledge," which he later formulated
explicitly: "[What makes us act] is merely the *latest*
outside influence of a procession of preparatory influences

stretching back over a period of years. No *single* outside
influence can make a man do a thing which is at war with
his training. The most it can do is to start his mind on a
new track and open it to the reception of *new*
influences. . . ."[13] Huck's "training" is in drama. The
single outside influence is his weeks, off and on, with
Jim, and the effect of this influence is his vow to steal
Jim. The new track and the new influences—the approach
to the Phelps farm, the new identity there, the
reappearance of Tom—lead him far from that vow. Thinking
as he apparently does that he can easily translate his vow
into action, Huck is committing the "sin" or error of
setting himself up to be transcendent, to be beyond the law
of man and nature. The events of the ending, especially
its early events, give a sharp answer to Huck's temerity.

The ending may be divided into a preparatory and
transitional section (Huck's rebirth, Tom's reappearance,
and Tom's establishment of domination), which
irrevocably changes Huck's direction; the growth and
climax of the evasion; and "the end," in which Huck
tidies up loose ends and prepares for the future. The
transitional section is the most important and interesting
one, for once the evasion is established, it follows the usual
laws of drama. Huck's introduction to the Phelps farm and
his rebirth create an effect of shock; they throw Huck
off balance and suggest a different world in which strange
things can and do happen, like the reappearance of Tom
Sawyer and the glimpse of the lynching of the King and the
Duke. These events also prepare Huck and the major
characters at the farm, Aunt Sally especially, for the drama
to follow.

When Huck arrives at the farm he is still caught up in

the ecstasy of his dedication—"I reckoned I better start
in on my plan straight off, without fooling around" (chap.
31)—but within a few minutes he is reduced to mumbling,
"I didn't rightly know what to say" (chap. 32), and a few
paragraphs later he is a different person. What has
happened is that Huck has gone through what Kenneth
Burke calls an "abyss," a radical shift in identity. First he
is reduced to a death-like state by contact with the
unbearable reality underlying man's frantic succession of
dramas, with the added touch of the spinning wheel.
Then he is truly reborn on the level of his humanity, his
consciousness, though his body has maintained its
continuity across the abyss. (This continuity counts for
little because we are never given any sense of the physical
Huck except as a near-reflection of Buck Grangerford.)

Huck enters this transition abruptly, with the opening
words of chapter 32: "When I got there it was all still
and Sunday-like, and hot and sunshiny—the hands was gone
to the fields; and there was them kind of faint dronings
of bugs and flies in the air that makes it seem so lonesome
and like everybody's dead and gone. . . ." In describing
this atmosphere, Huck draws on the capital created in
the scene of misery at the end of chapter 1. The impact
comes in two waves. The first introduces the feeling of
sadness and the thought of death; the second, in the third
paragraph of the chapter, completes the experience of
horror through the use of Twain's obsessive image,
the wailing sound of the spinning wheel. The two-part
structure of the experience suggests Twain's later analysis
of traumatic shocks in terms of a brick's first being soaked
slowly and then disintegrating at a slight final touch.[14]
Between the two waves comes the description of the

Phelps farm, which is sound social history on one level but has more serious literary functions. The description stops the action (here the movement of Huck as center of consciousness) and provides a moment for the first effect, the impact of nature, to "soak into" Huck for a while, before the final shock of the spinning wheel. The elaboration and precision of the description serve not only to locate the shenanigans to come but to slow the pace of the action, which has been rapid for several chapters and especially for the last chapter. Like the Grangerford house, the Phelps house is isolated from humanity by "the woods" (the natural nonhuman world). It is a stage on which special events are to take place, but its modest appearance suggests that whatever takes place will not be as terrible as the Grangerford massacre.

The spinning wheel reasserts the reality that chapter 31 denies. Human events are controlled not by conscious, righteous decisions but by basic laws of existence and human need—that is, by something resembling the "Providence" that Huck ironically puts his trust in at this point. Despite unfortunate experiences at the Wilkses, Huck "goes right along, not fixing up any particular plan, but just trusting to Providence to put the right words in my mouth when the time come" (chap. 32). The words that "Providence" puts in his mouth are "Yes'm," as a reply to Aunt Sally's greeting, "It's *you*, at last!—ain't it?" "Providence," that is, turns out to be the laws of drama; Huck assents automatically to being cast, to the assertion that he is "you"—whoever that may be. He does not know who "you" is, and neither do we; but of course it cannot be Huck Finn.

Huck thus begins his rescue of Jim by consenting to the destruction of his own identity. This death is reinforced unobtrusively. He has already wished he were dead; and when the dogs start to attack him, he dies as surely as if they had killed him, because the person rescued from the dogs is someone else, Aunt Sally's "You." The moments of anxiety that follow ("I wanted to . . . find out who I was") are a kind of limbo that Huck must endure helplessly. He is now cut off completely from the shining moment of chapter 31. The ruling principles of change and activity, and of man's need to adapt himself to such a world, have reasserted themselves. "Huck Finn" and his resolution are in the past. Now he must do something else, which under the laws of drama means that he must be someone else.

When Aunt Sally exclaims, "It's *you*, at last!—*ain't* it?", she suggests less a simple case of mistaken identity than the fulfillment of a destiny that has been waiting for Huck. On a precognitive level Huck seems to have been waiting for it too; he comes out with that polite "Yes'm" before he can think. Huck is now ready for his rebirth, the emergence from limbo. The muddle into which his loss of identity has put him begins to resolve itself, first in general terms: he becomes an ordinary person, which, in the terms of his culture, means that he becomes an ordinary white person (blacks are not persons). This definition is indicated and tacitly accepted in the interchange, "Anybody hurt?" "No'm. Killed a nigger." By thus aligning himself with conventional (white) culture and denying the humanity of blacks, Huck formally completes the separation from the anarchistic humanist Huck of chapter 31.

Next Huck is reborn in specific terms. This is Huck's
ironic anagnorisis, a twist on the climax of the classic
Bildungsroman. Huck has finally "made it." He is one of the
quality, one of those who can spurn ordinary standards
and limitations (like those of friendship). When Aunt
Sally tells Huck who he is—"It's *Tom Sawyer!*"—he not only
accepts the situation realistically—"there warn't no time to
swap knives"—but seizes it joyfully—"it was like being
born again, I was so glad to find out who I was." Aunt
Sally's being the source of knowledge, the giver of identity,
is important. She is the center of the Phelps household,
the only household in the novel that we see operating
on a day-to-day basis, and the necessary scene of any
attempt to rescue Jim. By naming Huck "Tom Sawyer,"
she is not just telling him that he is *the* Tom Sawyer, she
is authoritatively telling him that to succeed in this little
closed world Huck must be *a* Tom Sawyer—he must be
an aggressive maker of gratuitous dramas. The elements of
the boy Huck Finn, even (or especially) the elements that
make him noble, are irrelevant to practical affairs. From
what we already know of Tom's habitual way of treating
Jim, Aunt Sally's statement promises ill for a neat,
self-effacing, humanitarian rescue, or for any rescue.

Some kind of rebirth is logical because Huck's feeble
performance since approaching the Phelps farm has made
Huckishness look painfully inadequate. At the same time
this particular rebirth is ironical because no amount of
naming Huck "Tom Sawyer" will ever give him Tom's
malice, ingenuity, and energy. As it turns out, the
irony is double, for Huck gives up the advantages of being
Huck (simplicity, practicality) and in return gains
nothing. As Huck becomes "Tom," we are reminded once

again of the unity of the human race under surface
differences. At the beginning of the novel Huck wanted
"him and me to be together" in "the bad place." Now,
they are "together" or one, in name, as they soon will
be together in the flesh; and as for "the bad place," by the
time Tom gets through with the Phelps household it is a
very reasonable facsimile of hell. The manner of
Huck's rebirth is also logical from the point of view of the
dominant subculture, Tom's world of the quality glimpsed
in the opening and now solidly reasserted. To this world
Huck can be reborn only as a Tom Sawyer; for Tom
to them is the norm if not the ideal of boyhood, and Huck to
them not only is legally dead but never existed in the
first place, except for a few months as the widow's
embryo Tom.

Huck's rebirth as Tom also determines the immediate
course of the novel. It commits him to *Sawyerismus* before
Tom arrives, and prepares the reader for Tom's literal
reappearance. Nothing can conceal the clumsiness of that
coincidence. The encounter must occur at some time,
so that Huck can test his recent development against Tom.
(Twain undercuts this point: he has Huck crumble and
disappear before he can be put to the test against Tom.)
And of course the two boys cannot meet again in St.
Petersburg. Huck "died" at Pap's cabin; Huck is terrified
of encountering Pap again; Huck is deeply involved with a
slave who believes that he never can return home, and
his home was Huck's too.

Though Twain does not bother to try to make the
apparition of Tom logical, he handles the event so that its
impact comes not when Huck encounters him on the road
but when he marches up to the Phelps house. The first
encounter merely prepares the scene for the second, formal

one. Here Tom is a god, or perhaps a devil. Whereas
Huck really was a stranger when he approached the
Phelps house but could only mumble until he was
given a familiar label, Tom is not a stranger but easily
persuades the Phelpses that he is, and thus becomes, in
the super-reality of drama, the central Twain character.
Even when Tom's "identity" is known, he still remains
concealed, more the stranger than ever. Huck is forced to
accept a literally false but grimly appropriate identity; Tom
forces the Phelpses to accept an identity false in every
way. Tom is neither literally nor figuratively Sid
Sawyer. Here Twain depends on the reader's supposed
memories of *The Adventures of Tom Sawyer*, for Sid appears
only there. Sid, the embodiment of sterile conformity
and caution, was the opposite of Tom in every way. Even
the spite and vengefulness that he shared with Tom
were made to look like mere nastiness in Sid. Behind the
mask of Sid, Tom can remain himself, keep himself strange
to the Phelpses, and do anything he wants. He struts
around the Phelps farm as Satan walks disguised and
arrogant around Eseldorf in *The Mysterious Stranger*. From
the reader's point of view the concealment of Tom behind
Sid identifies Tom with the conventional culture and
reflects Sid's and its hypocrisy. If the story returned to
St. Petersburg and Tom, necessarily, remained Tom, it
would be difficult to avoid renewing too much of the
atmosphere of *The Adventures of Tom Sawyer* and of the first
chapters of *Huckleberry Finn*. In *Tom Sawyer* the
atmosphere was not serious, and man could not be seriously
examined in it; in *Huckleberry Finn* the same atmosphere
was essential for the preliminaries but otherwise
irrelevant.

The reunion (or fusion) of Huck and Tom returns Huck

to the world of gratuitous drama that he rejected early in
the book, but which, with his growing experience, he has
been moving slowly back toward, especially in the
Wilks episode. What inevitably happens next is a struggle
for domination between the would-be dramatists, Huck
and Tom, and beyond that, a struggle between anarchistic
selfishness and the vision of ordered decency glimpsed
in chapter 31. It is a struggle that Tom wins easily.
This outcome is thematically a final comment on the
relative strength of good and evil in the world of the novel,
and structurally a preparation for the rest of the ending.
Chapter 34, and chapter 35 to a lesser degree, determine
what will happen in chapters 36–40, the core of the
"evasion" and the part of the ending that has exasperated
readers and critics more than any other. If the reader
accepts Tom's domination, and the process that leads to it,
he must also accept the antics that Tom initiates, so a
close look at chapters 34 and 35 is advisable.

The glimpse of the King and the Duke tarred and
feathered moves Huck later (when he is writing) to remark,
"Human beings *can* be awful cruel to one another" (chap.
33), and at the time to brood on the uselessness of
conscience. Huck's moral insight is admirable, to be sure.
It has provided strong evidence for critics who see
Huck's moral growth as the novel's principle of coherence.
But in the given situation—and everything in *Huckleberry
Finn* exists in terms of given situations—Huck's admirable
reverie has disastrous consequences for his relations
with Tom and Jim. To attack conscience, even if conscience
is unreasonable, is to attack responsibility; and for
Huck to tamper with his sense of responsibility in the
presence of Tom Sawyer is to lower himself to the level of

that psychopathic personality, for whom all that counts
are energy and charisma—"style." And most important, to
brood about cruelty and conscience is not to think about
other things. For his own sake and Jim's, Huck should be
thinking about practical things at this moment of all
moments. "We stopped talking and got to thinking." Huck
is thinking about abstractions, but Tom is thinking about
the practical matter of dominating Huck so that he can
control the situation at the Phelps farm. To dominate
Huck, Tom at this moment solves a crucial problem,
the problem of Jim's location.

This small incident puts Tom ahead of Huck. Tom stays
there for good. As he goes along, he maintains and
reinforces his advantage any way he can. Huck never
catches up, never can catch up. He is beaten at the start.
Tom approaches the problem of Jim's location "detective
fashion" and presents the solution in terms of a sharp
Socratic quizzing of Huck; he is thus able to show up
Huck as unfashionable and dense. Huck is overwhelmed:
"What a head for just a boy to have! . . . I went to
thinking out a plan, but only just to be doing something; I
knowed very well where the right plan was going to come
from" (chap. 34). When Huck does broach his plan, Tom
redoubles his attack. Tom does not bother to point out
the plan's obvious weak point, that continuing "down the
river on the raft with Jim, hiding daytimes and running
nights" would leave the final solution of Jim's problem
farther away than ever. No, Tom yields completely on
Huck's ground, the ground of conventional practicality, but
attacks the plan and Huck on Tom's own ground, the
ground of real practicality, the ground of dramatic "style."
When Huck objects that nice boys do not steal slaves,

Tom will not argue that point either, and actually turns the situation to his own dramatic advantage by leaving Huck with the awed feeling that Tom has some mysterious quality that transcends the proprieties. "It warn't no use to say any more; because when he said he'd do a thing, he always done it. . . . If he was bound to have it so, *I* couldn't help it." Tom has raised himself to the awful level of a Colonel Sherburn. Tom clinches the matter by abasing Huck, forcing him to give *carte blanche* in meek reply to a harsh, repeated question:

> "Don't you reckon I know what I'm about? Don't I generly know what I'm about?"
> "Yes."

Tom has now shifted the basis of the rescue from Jim's simple need for freedom, into Tom's world, the world of gratuitous drama. Now Huck is reduced to ineffectual squawking, which Tom defeats with derision rather than argument; now the crazy logic of Tom's world shapes Huck's few "practical" ideas, like the suggestion that Tom should walk up the stairs and pretend they are a lightning rod. Huck's defeat is not the result of "his humility toward his own prowess" as a storyteller, as Richard Poirier puts it in *A World Elsewhere*; it is the result of his lack of prowess as a gratuitous dramatist, an occupation that involves much more than Huck's ability to tell stories in self-defense, that is, to create survival dramas.

Tom continues to control the situation and Huck, largely because he never lets up and Huck does. It is too easy to laugh comfortably with Huck at Tom's absurdities.

Huck misses the point when he condemns as "romantical" Tom's determination to climb the lightning rod. Tom makes it on the fourth try, thereby showing that he has the very important (and very Victorian) virtue of "sand," a virtue that Huck admired in Mary Jane Wilks. Tom's domination is clinched by his control of a crisis the morning after the lightning rod incident. When the boys enter Jim's cabin with Nat, the Phelpses' slave, Jim cries out with joy. "*I* didn't know nothing to do," Huck admits. But Tom coolly pretends that it was witches who spoke and even finds a moment to whisper to Jim. Later Tom similarly turns to advantage a potential crisis, "the hounds bulging in" under Jim's bed (chap. 36).

The wrangle about "the authorities" in chapter 35 also helps Tom to dominate. No obvious "practical" point is involved in these arguments, but Tom's stream of pedantries serves to upset and amaze Huck, and for Tom that is a practical effect. The tactic that worked with the boys in the cave works well again. In both cases domination of the situation is the aim, and domination is achieved. Huck cannot argue about the "authorities" on literary grounds, because he knows nothing about them, as Tom realizes. Neither does Huck, with his easygoing temperament, like this kind of jangling argument. Tom knows that very well, so he goes on and on with it. By citing irrelevant "authorities," *ad nauseam*, and by forcing Huck to listen to such nonsense and wrangle fruitlessly about it, Tom again demonstrates and solidifies his power. Were Huck learned in books and really skilled in dialectic (his earlier triumphs over Jim do not count), Tom would adopt another tactic. The means are secondary to the end, domination and its inexhaustible satisfactions.

There is another important benefit of all this for Tom. Huck is made more and more willing to *do* anything that Tom wants to do or wants him to do; any action is a relief from talking and from Tom's relentless verbal pressure. "You're always a-wandering off on a side issue," says Tom, with *Alice in Wonderland* logic. "Why can't you stick to the main point?" And Huck is reduced to saying, "All right, *I* don't care where he comes out, so he *comes* out; and Jim don't either, I reckon" (chap. 35). As Huck's comment shows, the feelings of Jim do not matter at all by this time. Tom has won. His drama casts Jim as a prop (the right role for a culturally defined nonhuman to play). In the most vivid way these sequences in the early parts of the evasion provide "prudential knowledge" of the tactics of power politics.

IV

Tom's perfect gratuitous drama is now well-established. All that keeps it from lasting thirty-seven or eighty years (Tom's ideal on different occasions) or two years (his grudging compromise) is, Tom thinks, the rate of Uncle Silas's activity in advertising Jim for sale. As Tom fails to realize, however, his drama, like any other, is shaped by its own needs and by the general laws of drama. It cannot be static; it must be active and constantly growing. Tom's domination of Huck is also not a static thing. It requires constant attention from Tom, and an endless round of activities to keep Huck busy. The result is that the evasion expands until it generates its own antithesis, the farmers' posse, the actual moment of counter-pressure being hastened by Uncle Silas's final move to advertise Jim in St. Louis. In this expansion first Nat is involved, as we have seen; then Aunt Sally and the whole Phelps household are entangled. Tom ignores Uncle Silas, who is so inane that he has no discrimination and cannot properly appreciate drama. Aunt Sally, however, is at the center of things and must be assimilated to the drama. Fortunately she is drama-hungry, as we learn from her rapturous interest in the man who died horribly after a steamboat explosion: "They say he was a sight to look at" (chap. 32). Tom is seldom more masterful than in his operations on this receptive, malleable personality (chap. 37). By degrees, by stealing shirts and sheets and silverware and putting them back and taking them again, he brainwashes Aunt Sally and turns her into his complement, a maniac who accepts anything, no matter how anomalous.

"So we was all right now," says Huck (chap. 37), realizing the possibilities of the situation and identifying himself with Tom, as he identified himself with the King and the Duke in their great days. Tom is so careful with Huck that Huck is largely content. When the case-knives are seen to be inadequate, Tom shrewdly yields a minor point and uses picks rather than risk a real rebellion, but maintains his control over Huck by forcing him not only to accept the pretense that picks are case-knives but to take part in creating the pretense. Tom asks for a case-knife; Huck hands him one; Tom drops it and repeats, "Gimme a *case-knife*" (chap. 36); Huck takes thought and hands Tom a pickax. Huck is left not just beaten but admiring: "He was always just that particular. Full of principle." A few hours later, Huck, now fully Tom's creature, *volunteers* the idea of letting the stairs stand for the lightning rod.

By this quick-wittedness and activity Tom keeps Huck
well in line. After Tom handles the crisis of Nat and the
hounds, Huck says with relief and satisfaction, "That was
all fixed" (chap. 37). The sequence that follows—the
preparation for the witch-pie—and some of the other
activities—making the pie, "smouching" the grindstone—are
described in a style distressingly reminiscent of the
style used for Huck's great drama of survival, his escape
from Pap's cabin: "We fixed it up away down in the
woods, and cooked it there; and we got it done at last, and
very satisfactory, too; but not all in one day; and we
had to use up three washpans full of flour before we got
through, and we got burnt pretty much all over, in
places, and eyes put out with the smoke" (chap. 37);
and, "So he raised up his bed and slid the chain off
of the bed-leg, and wrapt it round and round his neck, and
we crawled out through our hole and down there, and
Jim and me laid into that grindstone and walked her along
like nothing; and Tom superintended" (chap. 38).
Tom may well superintend. He has succeeded in releasing
Huck's drive to participate with others in activity—the basic
human drive that creates man's world. Though many
times frustrated by bullies and bunglers like Miss Watson
and the King, Huck retains this basic instinct, lets it out
a bit in the Wilks episode, and finds a perfect outlet
for it in Tom's schemes.

Tom's control and the elegant balance he has created are
soon lost as the need for dramatic activity drives him on
and drives Huck to follow. Tom bullies Jim, devises more
and more fantastic schemes, and at last gives Huck
little to do, thus ensuring the eventual onset of boredom.
It is at about chapter 38 that the whole affair becomes

too much for the characters and for patient readers,
even though it is still all quite logical in terms of the laws
of drama. The foolishness of the boys is now largely verbal;
the activities are simply more and more fantastic variations
on the same dramatic concept of the model prisoner. The
affair has become cancerous, out of control, because of
the insatiable demands of drama. Tom is in much the
same situation as the King and the Duke when they pass
the zenith of the Nonesuch. None of this is apparent to
the three inside the drama. When Tom calls Jim "a
prisoner of style" (chap. 39), he has no idea that the phrase
applies ironically to himself and to Huck as well as to
Jim. When Jim stubbornly refuses to keep rattlesnakes
(chap. 38), Tom suffers one of his few defeats; but neither
Huck nor Jim refers to the snake motif that has run
through the novel, and Tom has no way of knowing about
it. The escape of the garter snakes (chap. 39), the last defeat
by snakes, suggests the maddeningly evasive nature of
reality, which even Tom cannot control in the long run, but
no one sees the ominous portent. Huck simply remarks,
"I minded the trouble we had, to lay in another lot" (chap.
39). As in his early adventures with the King and the
Duke, Huck has been swept into uncritical identification
with the excitement.

All of the trouble is meaningless and irrelevant on the
practical level, not that that means anything to Huck now
or to Tom at any time. The drama that is "real," in
terms of the culture, is going on in the mind and actions of
that apparent bumbler, Uncle Silas, as he advertises for
Jim's owner and reacts silently to the lack of replies. The
relative value of the boys' and Uncle Silas's dramas is
seen when the old man says quietly that he will advertise in

the St. Louis papers and Huck reacts violently: "I see we hadn't no time to lose" (chap. 39).

Stimulated by this external catalyst, Tom's drama, which has been growing at a slowly increasing rate, now follows the pattern of the Grangerford and Wilks episodes. It fulfills its potential with a speed and violence that seem impossible until one realizes that this chain of events is following established laws. Some of the materials even have precedents within the novel: dressing Jim up like a girl recalls the Loftus incident (Jim's idea and also a failure); the "nonnamous letters" parallel the notes sent by Huck to Mary Jane Wilks or the note from Harney Shepherdson carried by Huck to Sophia Grangerford. The exponential increases in size and intensity have their reasons and parallels too. The Grangerfords measure the success of the feud in terms of the number killed ("right smart chance of funerals," says Buck); the Wilkses' neighbors see excitement as a function of the size and noise of the crowd, and reject the real Wilks heirs for promising to reduce both and return everyone to unbearable tranquility. When Huck asks Tom why he must write the letters, Tom says, "If we don't *give* them notice, there won't be nobody nor nothing to interfere with us, and so after all our hard work and trouble this escape'll go off perfectly flat: won't amount to nothing—won't be nothing *to* it" (chap. 39).

Tom's idea of "giving notice," the sending of the "nonnamous" letters, parallels Harney Shepherdson's sending of the anonymous note *"Half past two"* (chap. 18), or Harvey Wilks's asking about the mark on Peter Wilks's chest. In each case a small stimulus releases enormous latent cultural forces waiting for the dramatic

vehicle that will produce an apocalypse. Harney's
three words lead to a massacre, the logical end of the feud;
Harvey's suggestion allows the mob to take control and
move rapidly toward the supreme southern dramatic
climax, the lynching of everybody. Tom's letter provokes a
response that he cannot anticipate because he has
never encountered it and because he is too deep within his
culture to imagine it. His mysterious allusion *"Trouble is
brewing"* and his specific statement *"There is a desperate
gang of cutthroats from over in the Ingean Territory going to
steal your runaway nigger tonight"* touch off a panic
connected obviously with the Deep South's paranoid fear
of slave insurrections. Tom's instructions in the second
letter call for no more than one or two people to lock the
cutthroats in Jim's cabin, but "fifteen farmers, and
every one of them had a gun" (chap. 40) are what
Huck encounters when he goes into Aunt Sally's sitting
room the night of the evasion.

Huck realizes Tom's error at once: "I did wish Aunt
Sally would come, . . . and let me get away and tell
Tom how we'd overdone this thing, and what a thundering
hornet's nest we'd got ourselves into, so we could stop
fooling around straight off, and clear out with Jim before
these rips got out of patience and come for us"
(chap. 40). Huck fails, however, to recall a further law of
drama, that only accident can keep it from its logical
climax. No male Grangerford escaped the slaughter. Huck
escaped the Wilks debacle thanks only to a sudden crisis
and bad weather. Only a few scraps of luck save the
boys here: it is dark, the hysterical farmers shoot badly and
make too much noise, and the Phelps dogs do not bother
their friends the boys. The bullet in Tom's calf

is in a sense a gesture from the fates that rule drama, a
cuff from the mother cat telling the kitten to watch its step.
Tom, caught up in the hysteria, cannot grasp the
meaning of the wound, but Huck expresses the idea well
when he tells the doctor, "He had a dream . . . and it
shot him" (chap. 41). "Singular dream," says the doctor,
aptly, for Tom's dream was the dream of the perfect
drama, one that would end in perfect success rather than
collapse and bloodshed. Twain does not face the
issue as squarely here as he does a few years later in *A
Connecticut Yankee*, where Sir Boss's colossal dream-drama,
the remaking of medieval England into his version of
modern America, ends in a chaos of bullets and blood.

Huckleberry Finn does, though, have a splendid absurd
final gesture of its own—Jim's surrender, in which
he becomes a "white man," a southern man of honor, a
veritable Grangerford. It is Jim's one chance to play a
public role beyond the necessities of survival drama (in
which he did well as a recaptured runaway and a "sick
Arab"). He does it splendidly. And Jim's action, as the
reader can see even if Huck cannot, is also a dramatic and
existential triumph over the demands of his situation.
He knows the fate of the escaped, hunted slave in the Deep
South, and he chooses, in effect, to die in "style" and in
his own way, rather than messily and undramatically.

V

Since no one can remain on a high level for more than
a short time, Jim, in the last chapter, falls back into the
mass of humanity. Driven by the common human yearning
for aesthetic completeness, he accepts Tom's forty
dollars as proof of his prediction that he will be rich

because he has "hairy arms en a hairy breas' " (chap. 8).
The rest of the final pages find Twain likewise falling
back on tradition, the literary tradition of the *deus ex
machina*, to clear up the remaining loose ends so that he
may expeditiously reach what interests him, the last
paragraph of the book. This rapid forward thrust involves
Twain in some clumsiness, most of all the handling of
the brief disclosure that Miss Watson freed Jim in her will.
The disclosure itself is absolutely necessary, in order to
put Tom's behavior during the evasion into the class of
pure gratuitous drama, and to destroy any lingering sense
of moral authority; the point is, moreover, in character
for Miss Watson, as a dramatic gesture (see above,
pp. 129-30). Though Twain does allow Tom to make the
announcement of Jim's freedom into a little performance
in itself, and has Tom define gratuitous drama ("I wanted
the *adventure* of it") in reply to Aunt Sally's obvious
question, he hurries over the episode as he hurries over
the straightening-out of identities and the announcement
of Pap's death. It is all just a necessary bother to him.

Twain's real goal is to set up the ending in terms of
the impression of its structure. He manages to make
"The End" a triple end. It is "The End" of Huck's
writing, as the first edition shows, with its picture of a very
boyish Huck doffing his straw hat above the caption
"THE END. YOURS TRULY, HUCK FINN."
This is the writer's conclusion, underlining his statement
in the last paragraph, "So there ain't nothing more to write
about, and I am rotten glad of it, because if I'd a knowed
what a trouble it was to make a book I wouldn't a tackled
it, and ain't agoing to no more" (Chapter the Last). These
are the phrases that remind us that the novel is Huck's

own lyric cry, his struggle to say something about
existence as he knows it. By saying "a book" he reminds
us of what we have just seen and of its existence as a
solid, successful gesture, similar in kind to "the *adventure*"
for which Tom strives so hard, but enormously greater in
degree. Huck may well stop writing; he has proved himself
superior, in the last analysis, to Tom Sawyer, and after
that what is there left to do?

If we move back from Huck the writer to Huck the
character, we find him equally conscious of "a book,"
that is, of taking an overview of his experiences of the
past year. We arrive with him at the final sentence, "I
been there before," given as the reason why he must "light
out for the territory ahead of the rest." The four words,
"I been there before," have the whole weight of the book
behind them. "There" is the world created by, and
contained in, the book. With our experience of that
world we can accept the brief, unsupported statement.
Huck had to persist with his labor and "trouble" so that he
could write those four words and make us accept them.

Thus in one sense the novel comes to a satisfying formal
conclusion because the aim of the novel, the projection
of Huck's reality, has been achieved. This is not exactly
the same as saying, as some critics do, that the novel
reveals Huck's "growth," or did reveal it up to the clownish
final episode.[15] In terms of "growth" the last chapter
is dismal. It shows that though Huck may reject
"civilization," a certain set of patterns that put pressure on
him without rewards in return, he nevertheless accepts both
the general qualities of culture, the human way as he knows
it, and certain patterns for realizing cultural values.
The whole chapter, except for the paragraphs on the

death of Pap, is about drama; it opens with Tom's plans
for taking Jim back to St. Petersburg in style, continues
with the Phelpses' stylish treatment of Jim and his gloating
over the fulfillment of his predictions of wealth, and
goes on to Tom's plan for "howling adventures amongst
the Injuns." Huck accepts Tom's proposal ("all right,
that suits me") and the whole sequence; there is much
more accepting than rejecting of Tom in the chapter. As
for any improvement in Huck, there is no evidence of it.
His only objection to Tom's scheme is that he does not
have enough money to go along with Tom. When Huck
learns that he is still rich because Pap is dead, he makes
no comment at all—the question of money is closed,
and he has no feeling, no gladness or sorrow or relief,
about Pap's death. At the beginning of the novel Huck has
a flat, practical, anaesthetic temperament; at the end
he still does. "The territory" is not a place; it is a huge
blank by definition, being off-limits to whites in Huck's
time and in the 1880s. "The territory" promises nothing
except potentialities and absence of form, plus trouble.
Huck remains what he was in chapter 1, an ordinary
situational man, with no positive desires. His restlessness
here repeats his restlessness at the end of chapter 1. In
his day-to-day life he remains doomed to be pushed
around by the Tom Sawyers, those who have strong drives,
who want to organize life dramatically and need material
and accomplices.

At the same time Huck triumphs over Tom and the rest
of the mad dramatists. They can use him, but he can
describe them. Their dramas are temporary, and are
carved out of the uncontrollable medium of reality; Huck's
dramas are permanent, and are carved out of the difficult

but rewarding medium of language. When Huck says he
"ain't agoing to [write books] no more," he is perfectly
sincere; but he lives in a turbulent situational world, and
given sufficient need—the kind that he feels at the
Phelpses after the evasion—he may "tackle it" once again.
Art is always available, as it was for Twain in the crises
of his own life.

When Jim says that he will be rich because he has
"hairy arms en a hairy breas'," he goes on to explain why
he must believe that: "You see, maybe you's got to be po'
a long time fust, en so you might git discourage' en kill
yo'sef 'f you didn' know by de sign dat you gwyne to be
rich bymeby" (chap. 8). Huck's book is his "sign." It is
the sign that he has the means to be "rich" in the way
that counts in his world and counted for Twain—not, that
is, in terms of money, which Huck had at the beginning of
the story and which gave him no psychological benefits,
no real "profit," but in terms of the security that comes
from ordering the turbulence of reality and from the
demonstrated knowledge that one can order it. In this
security, rather than in Tom's frantic and ultimately useless
scrambling, lies what power a man can have. That is why
Huck can relax at the end and let Tom do the planning
and worrying. There may be, as Fitzgerald said, no second
acts in American lives, and Twain himself in later
years had to worry about the loss of his artistic potency;
but Huck, as a timeless projection of that potency, has
no anxieties about himself and the future that cannot
be handled in some satisfactory way.

1. *Mark Twain at Work*, pp. 91, 89.

2. Dictation of 30 August 1906, in Bernard De Voto, ed., *Mark Twain in Eruption* (New York: Harper, 1940), p. 199.

3. Preface to *The Aspern Papers*, in R. P. Blackmur, ed., *The Art of the Novel* (New York: Scribner's, 1934), p. 172.

4. Ronald Paulson, *The Fictions of Satire* (Baltimore: Johns Hopkins University Press, 1967), p. 43.

5. *The Sense of an Ending*, chap. 1 and passim.

6. Ibid., p. 28.

7. Ibid., pp. 164, 56, 19.

8. *Novel* 2 (Fall 1968): 14.

9. *The Fictions of Satire*, p. 69.

10. *Anatomy of Criticism*, p. 150.

11. Robert Scholes and Robert Kellogg, *The Nature of Narrative* (New York: Oxford University Press, 1966), p. 215.

12. *What Is Man?*, pp. 198-99.

13. Ibid., pp. 173-74.

14. Ibid., pp. 174-75.

15. E.g., *Mark Twain: The Development of a Writer*, pp. 114, 122 ff.; Marx, "Mr. Eliot, Mr. Trilling, and *Huckleberry Finn*."

The Dramatic Unity of *Huckleberry Finn*

Afterword

Huckleberry Finn and the Spirit of '77

Finishing *Huckleberry Finn*, a reader emerges from within
Huck's personality and blends afterimages of the ending
with a reawakening sense of the real American world.
From this process a final and larger meaning of the
novel begins to emerge. Twain does not articulate this
meaning nor does he prepare the reader for it; we are
dealing here with a cultural resonance of the work,
not with one of its internal qualities. I therefore call this
section an "afterword" rather than "chapter 5." From our
experience of Twain's dramatic world and of Huck's
vision of reality we can learn something of how and why the
Jims of America were and are treated shabbily by the
fictional and the real Hucks and Toms of America
then and now. Thanks to Jim's helpless involvement in
Huck's emotional cycle from involvement to boredom to
withdrawal, Jim is made to reenact the eternal human
drama of the victim and the American drama of the
nonwhite. It is not a conscious allegory of betrayal, but a

helpless illustration of the fact that some human beings betray and others are betrayed.

By the late 1870s and early 1880s, when Twain was working on *Huckleberry Finn*, he had grown beyond the mechanical topical novel and was working with a complex mixture of local color, southwestern humor, nostalgia, and myth; yet he was so completely of his era and his culture that when he stumbled into treating the extended relationship of a black slave and a white youth, at the very time (1876–83) that the nation was undergoing a fundamental shift in its relation to blacks, he could not help paralleling the national drama-sequence. In chapter 31 Huck would sincerely "go to hell" to free Jim; a few hours later he is thrown off stride by the situation at the Phelpses; a few hours after that he is easily seduced by Tom Sawyer into a grandiose scheme that uses the rescue of Jim as a means to an end; eventually Huck loses all but a spectator's interest in Jim. Rather like a group of genteel Hucks, the northern middle class, many of them former Radical Republicans who had fought to free the slaves, became irritated by the long bother of Reconstruction, became tired of southern hostility, and were easily seduced by strong-willed politicians and businessmen into abandoning the freedmen for new excitements like railroad building. In the crucial event, the Compromise of 1877, the Republican leaders traded withdrawal of the last troops from the South in return for the electoral votes of three southern states and continued control of the federal government. The spirit that led the country to accept the Compromise might ironically be called "the spirit of '77." Absorbed in his work and his new life in Hartford, Twain shared that spirit. He thought the Compromise a very good thing indeed. Three generations later the white civil-rights movement of the 1960s took a similar course: enthusiasm and dedication followed by loss of interest and absorption in new issues. "The spirit of '77" is still in us.[1]

Adventures of Huckleberry Finn is thus not only a great but a sadly typical American drama of race: not a stark tragedy of black suffering, but a complex tragicomedy of white weakness and indifference. It is one of those modern books that, as Lionel Trilling says, "read us," tell "us," Trilling's well-meaning, confused liberal Americans, about ourselves. In *Huckleberry Finn* Twain obeys Thoreau's basic rule, followed in many American masterworks, "to drive life into a corner, and reduce it to its lowest terms, and, if it proved to be mean, why then to get the whole and genuine meanness of it, and publish its meanness to the world." The meanness of *Huckleberry Finn* is not that man is evil but that he is weak and doomed to remain weak. This vision of man is embarrassing at best and unbearable at worst. As Stanley Elkins says of slavery, "There is a painful touchiness in all aspects of the subject; the discourse contains almost too much immediacy, it makes too many connections with present problems."[2] Twain did not shirk the presentation, but managed to avert his gaze from the subject's Medusa horrors by looking at it through his uncomprehending narrator.

However indirect Twain's method, *Huckleberry Finn*, including its ending, "speaks," as Barthes would put it, Twain's recognition of an American and a human dilemma and his acceptance of its painful difficulties. When Howells looked at Twain's dead face, he found in it "the patience I had so often seen in it: something of a puzzle, a great silent dignity, an assent to what must be from the depths of a nature whose tragical seriousness broke in the laughter which the unwise took for the whole of him."[3] In writing the ending of *Huckleberry Finn*, Twain made such an assent. By experiencing and accepting the ending we can perhaps take a step toward a similar level of self-awareness. A novel that can help its readers do that is indeed a masterwork and deserves its very high place.

1. The public events and feelings summarized here are well presented in C. Vann Woodward, *Reunion and Reaction: The Compromise of 1877 and the End of Reconstruction* (1951; rpt. Boston: Little, Brown, 1966); Kenneth M. Stampp, *The Era of Reconstruction, 1865-1877* (New York: Knopf, 1965); and William B. Hesseltine, "Economic Factors in the Abandonment of Reconstruction," *Mississippi Valley Historical Review* 22 (September 1935): 204-9. Woodward notes (p. 86) the resemblance between Twain's Colonel Sellers, of *The Gilded Age*, and Tom Scott, president of the Pennsylvania Railroad and a major force behind the Compromise; Tom Sawyer, though harder and much younger, has a good deal in common with Colonel Sellers. Twain's enthusiasm for the Republican cause in 1876-77 is abundantly clear in *Mark Twain-Howells Letters*, 1:143 passim. (In his old age Twain was stricken by the memory of the swindle of Tilden, the Democratic candidate, but failed to see it as a swindle of southern blacks also; see *Mark Twain in Eruption*, pp. 286-87.) In 1883, the year that Twain finished *Huckleberry Finn*, the Civil Rights Act of 1875 was declared unconstitutional, thereby opening the door for the final act of legal segregation.

2. *Slavery: A Problem in American Institutional and Intellectual Life*, 2d ed. (Chicago: University of Chicago Press, 1968), p. 1.

3. *My Mark Twain* (New York: Harper, 1910), pp. 100-101.

Index

Is Man?, 13, 14, 15; as central concept, 12-15; as tool for evaluating character, 18; controls Huck's attitudes, 16, 18; effect of, on concept of character, 18; effects of, on Jim's use of "honey" and "chile" to Huck, 27-30; in ending, 154, 172; in fog episode, 16

1601. See Twain, Mark, works by

Slave-hunters, as dramatists, 70

Slavery, as cultural drama, 61, 93; its painfulness, 191

Slavery. See Elkins, Stanley

Slaves, as dramatists, 99

Smith, Henry Nash, xi, xiii, 7, 19, 23, 47-48, 59, 79, 97, 108 n.26, 141, 146

Snakes and snakeskins, as structural device, 92, 133-34, 179

Solomon, Eric, 108 n. 25

Spinning wheel, auditory image of, 7-8, 11-12, 166-67

"Squshing," 5

Stranger, as archetypal Twain character, 6-7, 43, 99

Structuralism, xiv, xvi

Structuralism. See Piaget, Jean

"Structuralist Activity, The." *See* Barthes, Roland

Structure, of *Adventures of Huckleberry Finn*: and intensity of situations, 33-34; and lyrical novel, 131; as denial of conventional form, 111; as function of boredom, 32, 34-38, 41-42; as function of demand value of situations, 31-34; as parody of quest, 122-23; as parody of romance, 131; as three-part, 129; ending as formal conclusion, 184-86; generated by power

of drama, 67; in ending, determined laws of drama, 178-80; its cyclical nature, 32; of beginning (chaps. 1-8), 113; of central section (chaps. 8-31), 130-41; of ending, 153-56, 159-82; of "The End," 183-86; picaresque in, 155; place of episodes in, 124; relation of chap. 31 to ending, 164-66; relation of beginning to ending, 156-58; relation of middle to ending, 158-59; self-regulation of, 32-34; sequential nature of, 32; use of coincidences in, 160

Tanner, Tony, 6, 42, 102

"Temperament" (*What Is Man?*), as controlling element in man, 14

They Studied Man. See Kroeber, Alfred

Thompson, Laura, 5, 6

Thoreau, 191

Those Extraordinary Twins. See Twain, Mark, works by

Toward a Science of Mankind. See Thompson, Laura

Toward a Theory of Instruction. See Bruner, Jerome S.

"Town, the," as dramatic character, 74

"Training" (*What Is Man?*), as controlling element in man, 14

Tramp Abroad, A. See Twain, Mark, works by

Trilling, Lionel, 191

True Adventures of Huckleberry Finn, The. See Seelye, John

Turbulence, in world of *Adventures of Huckleberry Finn*, 5, 49, 145